Crusader-Woman

Ruxandra Cesereanu

❋

Saint Michael's Church, City of Cluj—*Photo by Ruxandra Cesereanu.*

Crusader-Woman

Ruxandra Cesereanu

❋

Translated by

Adam J. Sorkin

with Ruxandra Cesereanu,
Claudia Litvinchievici,
and Madalina Mudure

Introduction by Andrei Codrescu
Afterword by Călin-Andrei Mihăilescu

Black Widow Press is an imprint of Commonwealth Books, Inc., Boston, MA. Distributed to the trade by NBN (National Book Network) throughout North America and the U.K. All Black Widow Press books are printed on acid-free paper, and glued and sewn into bindings. Black Widow Press and its logo are registered trademarks of Commonwealth Books, Inc.
Joseph S. Phillips, Publisher
www.blackwidowpress.com

Cover Design by Windhaven Press
Cover Photo by Călin Stegerean
Book Design by Kerrie Kemperman

ISBN-13: 978-0-9795137-5-6
ISBN-10: 09795137-5-8

Library of Congress Cataloging-in-Publication Data

Cesereanu, Ruxandra, 1963–
    Crusader-Woman / Ruxandra Cesereanu. — Black Widow Press ed.
    p. cm.
    ISBN-13: 978-0-9795137-5-6
    I. Title

Printed by Thomson-Shore
Printed in the United States

10   9   8   7   6   5   4   3   2   1

Contents

Acknowledgments

All but the last of the poems in the section "The Fool of Delights" previously were published as part of *Lunacies* by Ruxandra Cesereanu, translated by Adam J. Sorkin, Ruxandra Cesereanu, and Claudia Litvinchievici (New York: Spuyten Duyvil/Meeting Eyes Bindery imprint, 2004), and are used by permission of the publisher, Tod Thilleman. Ruxandra Cesereanu, Adam J. Sorkin, and Black Widow Press express their thanks for permission to use these poems in *Crusader-Woman*. Individual translations first appeared in *The Marlboro Review* ("The Immaculate Woman" and "The Killer," together nominated for a Pushcart Prize) and in *Hotel Amerika* ("Ee-Hey-Na!" under the earlier title of "Bacchante Dancing," the poem not included in *Lunacies*).

Front cover photograph of Ruxandra Cesereanu ©2007 Călin Stegerean, used with permission.

An earlier version of Călin-Andrei Mihăilescu's afterword appeared in *American Book Review* and is used here with thanks.

Adam J. Sorkin wants to acknowledge, with gratitude, the support of Penn State Brandywine and the Penn State University College, as well as Institutul Cultural Român (Romanian Cultural Institute), Bucharest, for travel grants to Romania to work with Ruxandra Cesereanu on this book.

Foreword

Ruxandra Cesereanu begins her journey at the ur-ground of poetry, the beginning of the begots: "You are there, and I, here." This is from her "Letter to American Poets," written directly in English. "You are there, and I, here" is the first and last human utterance and the first and last line of poetry ever written. The Chinese poets applaud. Ruxandra's Here is Cluj, Romania, a medieval city where frozen stone knights stand and lie with Gothic stoicism in cathedrals, watching history coagulate, disintegrate, evanesce, and start again. Among them is a Crusader-Woman whose story the poet has elicited from dream and chronicle in a conversation that traverses the entirety of her flesh and blood. The Here of Cluj is stuffed with history and history's architectures, human types and phenotypes, and also with every imaginary escape (or escape into the imaginary) that was often (and is always) the only solution. The endless *dolor* of the unrelenting facts in their inescapable chronology has only imagination for an antidote, and that imagination (with channeled and glimpsed communications) must pass through death.

Cesereanu is a courageous poet. When she writes to American poets, she writes from her body because she is aware that for "American poets" the body is the chief currency of the realm. She wishes with all her heart to join them in their body with her body, because she imagines that America values history less than the future, the past less than the present. Brilliantly, the body she speaks from and offers us is not human, "A panther is writing you, American poets!" She has understood another fundamental aspect of America (or the poetics of), namely that America is truly and physically "post-humanist," that at its center is the animal self, nature. The defense of nature, the eco-centrist vision, is the secret of American poets and poetry. America, unlike Cluj, Romania, has the mission of defending nature with all its technological prowess, a paradox the poet knows well: "You are in the city traffic, with no Gods delivering," a line both awkward and obscure at first, until one realizes without a doubt that the traffic that prevents the Gods from delivering is also the inescapable reality from which Americans must escape. And here is where the panther, who kills and traffics only in night and hiding, bounds in to tear, rip, and heal. This panther was created from a technology of escapes and from bodies too numerous to count, from dark histories, from detours, from poetries that were extinguished. The Imaginary, the Hidden, the (maybe) Unreal, have their own dark ways around history: there is still stone in the stone Crusader-Woman of Cluj, there are still woods in her baroque palaces, the wind still whips around columns, the snow is mixed with the grays and red-blood of *isms*. Ruxandra Cesereanu knows them all, these byways of escape, these tunnels of rebirth. She knows also the art of inhabiting other bodies, human or animal, and she knows how to communicate from inside them with an intensity that is often wrenching. "Armor bursts open like a scar, / and the hearts of the ghosts, / the disappointed and the flayed boom like thunder. / The more you write, Scribe, the more you will die." Here are persons, one of whom is the poet herself, flinging themselves out of their various psychic or metal armor, to use language to agitate the ectoplasm, to mess with the neatly written chronologies, to throw the scribes' inkpots to the wall. Ruxandra Cesereanu travels to Hades and back many times in these poems, and not one of these journeys is frivolous.

Her poetics are traceable to the "Here" of Cluj, Romania, where the roots of her language draw from other articulations and dearticulated moans and sighs of a multi-lingual city, to the Surrealist poets, to the Romanian dream poets ("the oneirists"), and to the American eco-beat-rock 'n' roll poets of the "There" her panther leaps on. She begins in the stone (rock) of Cluj to make a flesh bridge to the music of there, the rock 'n' roll that liberated Eastern Europe from the tyranny of sloganeering. Cesereanu, make no mistake about it, is also a political poet, just like William Blake or Allen Ginsberg, just like Mina Loy and Alice Notley. She is a fierce dream visionary for whom only the transmutations of flesh to words to nature can save us from entropy and obsolescence. In her own English words, Ruxandra Cesereanu has introduced herself to American poets, but there is much more to be said, and these translations fling open the doors to all readers. The American poets to whom she has written her "letter" will doubtlessly welcome such a marvelous creature in their midst, and they will clamor, no doubt, for as prolonged a visit as possible. And they will fight over her kills. There is fresh blood here, folks, lick your chops.

Andrei Codrescu
Buffalo River, August 20, 2007

LETTER TO AMERICAN POETS

(Written directly in English)

❋

Cesereanu

LETTER TO AMERICAN POETS

I.

A panther is writing you, American poets,
men and women with knives and trees in your heart,
red teeth and violet tongues telling poems
about disemboweled solitude,
smoky days and Saturnian nights,
leaves and peppered harbors.
You are there, in the fountain of ashes,
I am here, in the highway of my brain,
trying to enter your heads through a warm surface,
playing the guitar and singing with my tobacco voice,
taking you near the moon in a game of hide and seek.
You have amnesia, I have amnesia,
we are both old flying through membranes and disasters,
while purple angels play trumpets
and the Apocalypse arrives sweet as a forgotten breeze.
I am pushing you up against the wall of lullabies,
shadowing sorrow, entering the yellow tunnel.
Hah, I am pungent and alone,
you are in the city traffic, with no Gods delivering.
I would have liked to feel your touch,
my young-old skin is disappearing in these noisy days,
but I am undamaged and unafraid
of yesterdays coming like beheaded queens.
You are there and I, here,
cyanotic gates are climbing on my bones,
I am writing about your lives and dark sides without knowing them,
only because from thousands of miles away
I smell rains and dreams as they are not.
The lizard of my poem gets you from within,
you are there and I, here,
but all of us tumbled in the big washing machine of the world,

with sunflowers for hearts
and landscapes of eyes as electric skies dancing lost rock and roll.
Hah, I would have liked to bend over America like a whirling
    dervish,
trembling bridges with my temples,
crossing stars with my hair,
breaking birds with my walls,
hot waves, hot waves in brains
and the ribs where an angel has fallen like a magician's hat.
You are there and I, here,
half human beings, half animals and another half objects of prey,
talking, scratching, drinking, remembering,
lying, thinking, searching, not finding,
knowing, flying, living and dying in the honor of no God.
A panther is writing you, American poets,
my fears are yellow water wings,
this is why I tell you I'm about to change in the alchemic sunlight,
buying at the supermarket all the things I need for my
    transformation:
little iron balls, a parrot, gentle darkness, jaws of void,
one scarface, wind veins, chlorine.
I am inside an interval of my life
where there is no shame, only a swollen repentance for nothing
and the abandoned windows of night
where I offer myself as a feverish skin.
Goddamn.
I need nobody because I have eleven fingers,
but I am not sorry
for my head is exploding in a hurricane
and my body drowns its little snakes.
You are there and I, here,
sitting in the bedroom of our lives with looking-glasses for bones.
A black-swan gaze in our eyes

and the sound of death as a necklace—this is what I feel.
But there is also the hard transparency of strangers,
the white nails of several ghosts in the very morning
while the silence slowly carries its corpse.
Yes, I would have liked to be a pool of dreams,
catching them like butterflies on the edge,
taming lunacies with my old guitar filled with shells.
You are there and I, here,
wasping and narrowing myself, blinding despair
(but what is blind despair today?),
vanishing space and time in a cup of coffee,
mourning about lost friendships and deep spiritual touches,
forgetting I'm just a poor human being like everyone else.
Goddamn, once again.
Inside my abdomen are all the obsessions I had
when I was a little girl playing in the mud with toys.
Once upon a time I walked to a tower in the forest
where I found no life.
I learned there about what love isn't and what I am not,
about death and why flies always buzz around us,
about the color of my brain between morning and midnight,
reminding me I'm just a mouth at dusk,
a failed nun and white flesh.
While the wheel of the world is turning its moods
I can say I am happy and unhappy,
a passenger between limbos,
missing dreams about God or Devil,
both like two ruby rings or two jaws
abandoning men and women and their remains in slow harmony.
You are there and I, here,
soul to soul, but not body to body,
recognizing the neighborhood of the heroine
when all is possible in the end,

understanding freedom as an empty room
where solitude is growing like mass destruction.
Let's sell diplomas for such hidden feelings,
in the name of dead kings whose crowns are in museums and
    hospitals!
Let's photograph the size of stars,
deep in their flesh and shining blood.
Through my vision,
I saw a savage horse filled with the events of past and future,
silk dancing in the canyon just like the skin of alien grief,
but now I'm foggy-headed, I see no more,
I touch no more,
I eat no more, I dream no more,
I am banished and murdered as a challenged memory.
Goddamn, for the third time.
Do you think there's still time to live and write about it?
Do you think there's still time to watch a yellow-orange sunset,
finding your life deep in the entrails?
I don't think life is shit, but a railway.
The dark side of my moon is entering the shining side of my heart,
so this is why I'm falling into myself,
splitting words, cutting storms, shadowing gentle brains.
When I went to search for that tower I told you about
I saw all the animals in the dining room of the forest,
with sunglasses as if they were masters of the world.
The animals were playing Tarot cards
and in that moment I knew I was inside a dream.
How to escape from there? How to run?
I began to play with the lion, my master of the zodiac.
My lion had blue eyes and the melancholy of a salamander.
My lion overwhelmed me, a liquid form coming from my own body,
my lion was asleep and I touched him amazed,
because he was electric and I was trembling.

I was lucky to have such a master of the zodiac,
such a protector angel creeping in my head.
I knew I'd lost my innocence—
sometimes a rainbow beyond my control reminds me I'm human,
with my way, my life, my death whenever it will be.
This is the reason I like marriage ceremonies,
this is the reason I like imagining past and future centuries
as pink flamingos in a deep green lake.
You are there, paralyzed in your American oblivion,
I am here, crippled in my unfinished Europe,
angry with myself,
because I am trapped between limbos:
sisters of fear, men in the daylight of my childhood,
weeping dogs of my night, please come save me.
I don't want to die unwounded and untouched.
Surrounding hidden fogs, hypnotizing naked hermits,
feeling the silenced power of the eagle,
discovering frozen hearts in the garbage,
I need all these sensors to be alive.
Purple whispering tongues, crowded rooms with nervous ghosts,
a blackbird flying in my head as a breath,
this is what I am.
Until now, all my life, I tasted the void of the elevator to hell,
the deep breaking through,
hundreds of hands evaporating in the air like wings,
dark lovers chopping their passion to pieces,
a glimpse of solitude a dozen times revealed.
What more should I do?
I have my mind in a plastic bag.
Strange creatures smash the walls,
bridges and gates of the four elements and their boundaries,
here we are with a great pain in the stomach,
because of the idea of death,

her long teeth and gothic nails. Ha, ha.
Clouds in flesh, devouring veins,
while the carnival is never-ending
and the hair masks are curling for miles and miles.
Anxiety slowly slides in my pocket like a handkerchief,
anxiety, grief, desolation and so on.
I am playing rainy thoughts on the saxophone,
covering my face as in a prayer and struggling for reality.
We never drank together, we never smoked marijuana together
so as to disappear in dust.
I have windy spaces in my throat
when I write about the small desires of human beings.
But my words are not desperate, as I reject the filthy madness.
I stare at all these waves of warm things:
hands, legs, eyes, sex, bones, tails, etc.
My way is to describe and to feel them,
playing chess with God,
as he is not a bastard anymore, just wise marble to build fate.
I am not guilty to think of things as I do,
and if I am, Goddamn.
I am not losing my mind, I am not tricking myself,
but feeling too intense.
This is the risk of life and writing,
to hit too directly; even we are not fighters.
Holes of nowhere, nobody's memory, repentance of the void,
suicidal beings, it's hard to take the traces of all these,
not shaving their sense and goal.
What I want now is to play my guitar like a teenager,
without any consideration for the world,
just I, not awakened from my crazy mood.
Hello mother and father not exposed here,
hello friends staring at me like the crows of a shaman,
hello red love and red death of one dollar,

my internal chemistry is alien, but I like it, hah!
It is said that the Devil is God's monkey,
but I am sure now that the poet is the Devil's monkey,
so he is closer to God than to the Devil.
I feel like a schoolgirl writing here
about the many fences and walls I want to break,
about bruises and scars we can see on the windows
when all is impossible to cherish and love.
In this big hotel which is the world
there are cocoons and sailors and octopuses,
businessmen and drunkards, psychoanalysts and monks,
whores and beggars, wasps and saints.
What I want now is a Russian ice tea
and the music of some gypsies dancing like hell.
Where are our souls?
In what naked desert?
Nests of sand, from where the fuel of angels slides in the frightening
    grass,
I am mourning for you.
I want just to sit in a tavern,
wrapped in tentacles of voices, a flower of absinthe floating inside.
Skin echoes at the borderline of my brain.
Again and again I'm saying that you are there and I, here,
weeds and flames of the unconsciousness,
still melancholy is the chained queen of insomnia.
Long live this bitter insomnia
as another world is knocking at the door.
Enter, I say, enter and sit down.
To devour and to enslave, this is the question.
Wisdom is molded in its coffin
like a mad train that does not stop at any station.
The tongue of reality is so curved
that it can lick only the vibrations of emptiness.

Who wants to live? Who doesn't?
I would like to meet an emperor for all these feelings and moods
    and crimes,
to talk with him in a large banquet hall,
chewing our food like wise cows.
There is a constant scream of nothingness,
so it is obvious that only the wind hears the bubbles of despair.
Lace of the end, drowned thunder of the silence,
our vital organs are misty,
we are not sinners, not sinners,
only lanterns in the dark.
I have a bird in my throat, flying nowhere,
it's raining and the water is shining,
the bird is just an object of a thrilling imagination,
that imagination that we all feared as children.
Scratchy moisture in my mouth, fibers of solitude,
tattoos of a mistaken happiness, corridors of flesh and blood,
here is the church where priests no longer talk to God, but to
    UnGod.
Vacuum of the edge, lights of ribs dancing over Europe
as monkeys project a movie about how they will disappear.
Let's throw clothes, let's switch,
down with the time of frozen surfaces,
now is the time of twisted silk on a bridge near heaven.
What a luxury of the abyss!
Yes, I hear the dolphin's song.

II.

A panther is writing you, American poets,
I am alive and purple, tricking nobody
with my eroded pain in words and sentences,

but this means filling reality with icebergs.
You are there and I, here,
and there is no emergency room between us.
The inner heart of all is elusive,
beating like a deep moon in the ocean.
The oxygen of self-consciousness is gone,
but I still trust in a kingdom without tears and hollows,
the survival of tumults.
I am a hunter and you are hunters too,
so let's think about how we can't be murdered
and let's endure the blood language.
We are not tamed, this is our link and crash.
Tunnels are always fascinating,
but inside there are strange dry lights, not returning to their home.
Desolation is delivered.
The voice of an animal screams through the mirrors,
struggling for life,
come back, I say, stay with me,
don't vanish and burn your lips—
nobody has the power to listen to a scream.
But the animal splashes my face,
it is a mad injection of the way to be full of yourself.
Once upon a time, I used to walk in cemeteries with my lover,
it was good there to taste death in the afternoon.
I was like a little stone on a grave,
my lover, a lightning nerve,
and we swam together in the lake of our young dying heart.
I saw the cemetery as our future world,
hanging like a fly in a spider web.
My lover was lying in the grass, speaking to the dead,
his unforgotten friends.
I learned to accept and to caress the void,
to be close to nothingness.

Not to give up.
To have the moon as my guiding shamaness.
To have faith until the end.
To watch my strength fly from the orphanage and become
   a champion.
To grow sunlight from inside until it explodes tenderly.
I have the skill of an exorcist, I know that.
At carnivals, I'm always playing the Hangman,
because I like to suffer a little bit for the others,
to drink and hide for them,
to be bad and kill.
But this is just a shadow falling.
I would like to ululate, frozen in the night.
Everybody needs camphor for their wounds,
but when the wound is in the thinking skull,
the camphor is just a warning to think deeper.
I invite you to sit down, American poets,
to tell me how is it inside a coma,
how many wonders do you have in your crazy dreams,
how you tie your fate,
how about emptiness?
You are there, I am here with my snake hair,
twirling you around like healing human beings,
praying for a holy fog to come
together with the perspiration of darkness
when nothing survives under the full moon.
I am infected with a yellow fever,
this is the reason I'm deepening the gap between myself and yourself.
But I smile even in the face of catastrophes,
because I know who I am.
Face to the desert, I have the burning shape of a coyote,
face to the ocean, I am a whale without eyes,
face to the sky, I am the secret history of the green grass,

face to myself, I am a violet mouth.
Probably most of this poem is delirious,
but this means only that I cut the surfaces in rays.
My teeth are running in a car race against time
since they lost their childhood and paradise.
Together with my teeth, I have learned to be numb, to be scared,
    to whisper.
I have never dreamed of wings, but I flew over unknown cities,
sprinkling salt on their icy towers,
understanding the glamour of the invisible.
My cave was at the corner of the sky,
a sort of jellyfish Fifth Avenue for non-abandoned minds
from where it is possible to enter a velvet waterfall.
All this is circus.
I already said I want to heal,
but who needs healing?
Only in despair can we keep and witness reality
without the map of the body.
To bump into other bodies as ghost ships.
Once upon a time we were born.
To fight against things like a lunatic throwing himself out the
    window.
To be dragged by the machine gun of times.
To dive in brains for love and hate.
To hemorrhage missing feelings about collapsed hearts,
these are waves and hidden hollows about how not to be and not
    to die.
Under eyelids, a shroud of naked ice.
Can we say we are still alive?
Monks have open mouths for the key of Heaven,
but also the winter skin of blind men.
I am not sure that they have not lost the path.
To survive drowned in black wine,

to see memory as a dog near the house
or as a big fire enslaved by strangers who don't know what to do.
A sword of water running on the fire
and the rainbow's mind like a bridge to nowhere.
Clowns we are in the moonlight,
buried by a never-ending fury.
I found beaks in my room,
like knives for twisting eyes.
The path is absent and the spices not good.
I am the taxi driver of my life.
Trainspotting is the method,
entering in the water-closets of shadow.
I try to seduce the bridges to the End,
I try to remember the unknown till death is not here,
I am smiling and distilling fears, but not crying,
never returning to harmony.
The doors of frustration are always open.
I would like to smoke a cigarette with God,
just the two of us, fresh and lacking hypocrisy.
I am a teller and a winner, let's hope,
punishing despair.
Wishes are not bad, but mad,
fingerprints on the moon,
kisses on the skull,
steps in the broken mind.
Who am I? Who are you?
I forgot the lonely song of the she-wolf,
but I know the zigzag of how to run far away from the world.
At dawn, I like to drink coffee with my night-dreams.
I speak to the dream characters,
my daughters moving so fast, dying in speed,
dissolving my head like gasoline pumped on a highway for the
    explosion.

Change is a cryptic flower with lips and skins.
The fall is a stubborn witness in life,
stubborn as a pendulum in a trance.
The prophets are in the hospital.
I am living and I am not lost.
And I want to change myself.
Speaking about awareness,
whoever listened to the whistle of down
when faith is so lonely, like a chess-game without players?
Whoever climbed darkness until turning into a winged messenger?
Whoever smelled the aroma of dangerous landscapes
that make you need a killer instinct?
Yes, we are predators and for us indifference is just the relic of a
    forgotten saint.
Frozen clock, wild razors,
a puzzle of hair, the pilgrimage of colors,
these are all signs that astronomers will come to understand,
if paranoia has not conquered the illuminations.
Anything can be nothing,
because chaos has the skill of a challenged sanctuary.
Madness has no crucifix and no regrets.
I executed Beauty like a torturer beating a tapestry,
seeking for its blood ballet.
There are no oracles today, just asylums with a menthol taste.
I am looking for the undecipherable underground
as a stranger longing for his enigma and orange resurrection.

III.

A panther is writing you, American poets,
cutting ice in brains on fire,
wearing bracelets of midnight hair.

You want to know if you are still alive?
You want to find the truth so as to be saved?
Denial is a good answer for deaf mutes.
I move in your entrails like a submarine,
without gloves, without birds in a cage,
just my narrow body and mind,
just the shadow of a thunderstorm
telling the story of the human being and his time.
Rain is a big tear in coma for deeper thoughts,
so don't look back,
just enter the corridors of the burning house
and find there a blind horse with a crazy diamond.
Flying tattoos and scars and black holes,
surreality is not enough after a hard time in hell.
But reality hangs from the walls like a widow.
Crippled swans bathe in it.
Why are miracles like junkies today?
Why are names not open doors?
Why are cocoons no longer little churches in skirts?
To behead dolls is just a way not to be bored
and it is not a demented mood for aliens.
Whispering flames, waiting for the God of butterflies,
I am here, standing in front of my death opening flesh.
Sand and hallucinations are conquerors running to the breakthrough.
I am not spitting on my fate, but eating and sucking it.
I am very carnivorous with you and with myself,
translucent like a ship with veins.
And I can't make the sign of the cross anymore,
because I am not a bride, but a woman.
I saw electric corpses far away,
where absence is a powerful law.
I saw the bruises of consciousness ride like nomads.
My heart is a mammoth having his life in fur.

I forgot the sense of sorrow,
I forgot the fluid pains
and the blessed sins of everybody darkened by vows.
Our world is a harmonica,
so, sweet monsters and shining beasts, please sing and dance,
sing for the redemption and the bulimia of today.
Shrinking a palimpsest.

IV.

A panther is writing you, American poets.
Cheap night, cheap day, come with me where there are no questions.
Following the fog, licking the windows, falling on sleeping terraces,
I wonder if I have a pool inside my brain
or I was born in a pool with many mothers swimming.
There is no time for such spiritual murders,
so I turn back from outside,
as inside my hair is a stairway to heaven.
I am not rich, but I like to disturb the world.
I have measured so many mornings of my life with a knife
that now I can say I am not at all delivered to a Savior.
Perfumed shrouds at dusk,
silenced serpents coming from the pipes,
how can I not be afraid of the lonely prophets
if they show their fingers with five rings of gold!
I would have liked to come back from the dead
in a sweet sunset of my thirties,
smoking a cigarette, talking to Nobody,
overwhelming the streets with my new body and soul,
hip-hip-hurrah, I came back from the dead,
wish me good luck, my friends!

This is not the moment for such a resurrection, Un-God would
    have said.
Go back to your death,
you have no human voice, no human blood or nails,
go back to your death,
wintering your entrails,
go back, go back.
It's midnight and I am alone in a masquerade,
a newspaper on my head,
with my muddy consciousness,
a dozen sordid sins I have never done
are picking my skin.
Once upon a time I was alive like a laughing mouth,
the fuel of my memories is burning the eyes,
the orange eyes of a yellow cat.
I am no longer young, but not entirely old,
just waiting between, in a room without windows or doors.
Does any fool remain to mock the mysteries?
Does any young king remain to live naked in the middle of
    his people?
Does any body wish to be more than flesh and blood?
Bodies of water, fire, air and earth,
bodies of East, West, South and North.
Guests of silk arising from obscurity with vain desire,
who can say that indifference is not our dearest queen,
the best, the oldest, the loneliest.
I think everyone today could be his own hangman.
Pouring waters on our heads,
cleaning flesh and anti-flesh,
washing our legs with black nails,
does purification still mean anything?
Everybody has a hermit-shadow,
a sort of endless brother in the Unreal.

A violet twin or a lighted wing in the horizon,
making signs about strange times and rains.
A chapel of monk bones
surrendering the battle for glory.
Things are blessed if it's possible to be blessed.
Things are powerful only if power has renounced its kingdom.
No mercy for the infirm eagles:
if you eat their liver you will live forever.
Is this what you want?
Shining. Frosting. Not agonizing.
I inherited the long way to forgetfulness.
Despair is my beloved mother and father,
like the toothed mouth of a shark,
as I don't trust in the unspoken Redemption.
Cursing the years, the deep days melted with darkness,
grumbling at the journeys outside,
sitting in a tavern and drinking the liquor of an alien death in ecstasy.
Cutting wonders and whispers and ghosts
in a house with drunkards,
caressing the forgiveness of passengers with fearing eyes,
I think we need only a big confusion to live anymore,
to want to live and believe in something.
Corridors inside the moon are like a human brain,
I am walking on these corridors with some little passion,
some little courage (but very little) and a strong weakness.
No devils on my back, but also no angels,
just Me and Myself,
an endless delirium excited and shrilled by its taste,
a fornication of nothingness on a spring day
when green received its coronation once again.
I don't know what it is to be dishonored.
Lilac feeding my heart,
bones drinking the blackest coffee I ever knew,

feeling my freedom like a stone,
I am the ivory daughter of man.
I remember I played Tarot cards with some shadows last night
and my horoscope was not wise.
But I liked seeing my death and the Unreal.
Speaking about the Unreal,
it is a burned house, with wings of desire,
where I feel myself a panther!
But it could be also a forest
where a bloody blind nightingale is singing:
what is life? what is death? stop.
what is lifedeath? stop.
who are you? who am I? who we are? stop.
I want to speak not to the desert,
but to someone alive, to touch his or her mouth,
thinking that nothing is unforgiving.
But it is really nothing unforgiven?
Nothing, nobody, nowhere.
Where is the Death we have lost in dying?
Where is the Birth we have lost in being born?
Where is the God we have lost in God?
Or the UnGod?
I am a stranger. I do not understand.
I do not know. But I feel.
Pietàs petrifying more and more their liquids,
this is my memory.
We can say a lot of things.
I have the power to say.
The womb is large and lonely.
This is a landscape in rainbow.
This is a landscape with wombs.
I am a surgeon of beasts.
Is fornication still a sulfurous sickness?

Are the hollows wise paths in themselves?
Tabula Rasa and bubbles.
Cliffs and cages.
Amputation of absence.
Whistling for love with mercury on the tongue.
Skulls and money. This is our world.
The widows of the puppets shut the doors
and nobody can enter or leave.
My hair is schizophrenic.
I like mausoleums.
Breaking hieroglyphs and eternity.
Disinfecting the agony which murders.
I lost all miracles.
Horses in pain killed by pity.
I am working inside the blackness.
I am in the schoolroom of my soul.
I gave up the failure of grief.
I am a corpse. I know how to contain my death.
Will I ever find life once again?
My wounds have their earrings and bracelets.
Skin is everything, a hard skin.
I am on my side. I am inside.
Tattoos and desires.
Who can say that I lost purity and beauty?
Who can say I am slaughterhouse lightning?
My illumination is cold.
Ashes are singing.
What is the smell of a prayer?
I can do acupuncture on scars and stars.
My world, I hurt you because you hurt me.
It is like jumping into a mirror.
Opacity is cut by a sleeping axe,
I want to swallow every surrender on this earth.

To dance for a battle and for repentance
is not so easy at the beginning of the millennium.
Fetuses are lying near the broken walls.
I do not hate anybody, but life after death has strange coins
    and edges.
Maybe I have to go on a pilgrimage.

THE FOOL OF DELIGHTS

Cesereanu

THE IMMACULATE WOMAN

Inside you, woman,
your body is a stained glass window.
Oh, untouched night!
Mules, mimes astride their backs, ride into the station.
The skulls of violet prelates
line up at your feet and harmonize.
Far in the distance, the basilica is a ghost.
The wind from the steeple and the strumming of guitars
spread everywhere on the island.
Woman, your white spine is a lighthouse.
Tall and tearful, you tower
in night's cream-thick glow.
O, tiny mother of a single son,
always on the surface of time, venerated
by seven thousand unholy, lonely men.
Ave!
Your wolfram thighs
seem scissors for the unbelieving.
Writing of you, scribes clench their jaw in horror.
Your turgid scars balloon,
tired pilgrims scramble inside you,
and the moon whistles, the moon whistles.
Lacemaker you are, Mary,
dressmaker of saints.
Your deaf thighs jingle-jangle
in the ears of the much too worldly,
your womb of fog is a famous killer.
You saunter by, sinuous in a head nurse's uniform,
the scent of sleep lingering in your tracks.
White serpent,
you shed your sallow skin
as if slapping the winner's face
with the loser's banner.

It's you who become the prize trophy
when the hunting horn sounds,
a deluxe rabbit, soft and plump,
seven ova adorning your womb.
We catch your scent as you really are,
like a silver-haired pensioner in a jar of spirits at the museum.
You sleep in chloroform, Mary,
and I wait and wait for the elevator to take me up to Jesus.

—A.J.S./C.L./R.C.

THE KILLER

She can't. The woman. Can't.
The fish of her heart no longer breathes.
Its scales seep red, stain the moonlight.
She kills her machinery of birth,
her frenzied thighs rising as high as the sky,
her nights and days ripped to rags.
Sinful but alive,
light camouflaged under her skin like ground glass,
she stays in the tunnel.
A girl sleeps an arsenic sleep
in the emergency room.
Killer, I lick the oily heart's honeycomb from my lips!
Your face strobed by sleep's flicker,
you flee through the garden, smeared with rain,
and strike against the buoy.
Old tigress, you who kill behind bars, you've fled.
You know He can see you from aloft—
God the Plush, God the Slasher.
Like a mad nun, you wander,
your head pungent with blood,
deposits of blood you can smell
all the way from the kingdom of heaven.
The believers adore you with their eyes, tongues lolling,
drooling Pavlovian dogs.
Devoid of grace, you yourself are a topsy-turvy chapel.
You descend upon them like a spider at sunset.
On your bosom, black lilies.
Your teeth, white as tombstones,
purify altars and famed steeples.
The hooves of the murdered stampede over my body,

dripping musk, crippling me.
Killer, from your throat a dying city rattles its death rattle.
The silence grinds out luminescence in lambent silence.
I should sip champagne. Cross myself.

—A.J.S./C.L./R.C.

THE ANGEL ZED

Spiders without a cross
creep up my hands,
cadmium-selenium-sulfur red.
I let my hair down
and drowned myself,
a dark Ophelia beneath a parched, hoary willow.
I offered a silver basin and satin towel
to soften in musk
your hard, ancient claws.
The soothsayers prophesied just three nights more.
At dawn I saw my mother, a dream-bride.
Sick. I am sick.
My tongue, split by sleep,
my eyes, shriveled to their roots,
dying to disappear.
Your howls echo in vain, Angel Zed.
In my tendons I hoard two liters of crushed saints.
Nausea squeezes my memory in its vise.
My veins, like reservoirs, are flooded to the brim.
Slowly you drown in my body,
marshals of tar, priests of flesh!
If you want to be my lover-girl,
you must adorn yourself with a garland of nettles.
My hair smells of charred flesh:
look, how ugly the queen is, skin and bones!
I set off with what yet remains mine,
to complete myself as a woman,
hearing my body metamorphosed into an insect-nun.
Dead, Angel Zed, you are dead,
and your smoking head ponders miracles.
You have a heart of phosphorus,
death seeks to invade your glassy mouth
as a cloud of green stars.

Give me your name, man's last end,
give me your four eyes!
Deep inside you, mornings linger on,
where old butterflies alight, giggling.
You fill me with distance's flood, the five rivers of blood,
you caress my windpipe.
Heed only yourself, Angel Zed,
but don't forget your straw hat.
When it rains you whistle
through seashells in place of teeth.
You sleep inside yourself,
that God might flap the mouth in your head
when you bleed.
Silence perches in your depths like a beakless eagle,
bells awaken you for night's blackest hour.
The soles of your feet are a pair of mollusks.
Dogs know your smell from far away:
your eyes are putrid from the stench of the streets.
Softhearted orphans choose to take to their heels,
a white brilliance keeps you from hearing
their desolate cries.
I climb, I descend;
I see and listen to you tremble
at my animal passage.
You are as pure as a freshly made bed,
your lips are dried figs in the sand.
I hear the fall of blind night.
I drowsed while the blood seeped away,
and I didn't see you flying.
Then, in gelatinous sleep, I nibbled your mouth,
the cleft of your chin,
your rose-red left shoulder.

You wore the scent of snow,
you were a tattered rag of smiles.
Black raven circling round
high above my head.
Black raven circling round.
No, I won't be yours, dark bird.
The ax in my head cuts. Cuts.
The blood of my bleak solitude no longer can endure.
The Angel Zed is murmuring in my dead ear.

—*A.J.S./R.C.*

BESTIARY

Doors and lids burst open in my arsenic house,
a living house between my ribs.
At first some children, green with hatred, clambered out.
Crouched in my head. Hunched in my stomach.
Scratched on the windows.
The butterflies of the ear have disappeared
into a zone of the body I myself don't even know,
the second head, the seventh hand.
Anyway, the third eye is closed and jaundice-yellow.
An owl hatches a blind chick within its orb.
Just before dawn, the owl puts on dark glasses,
hoots once, *whooo,* swoops into the wall.
She could be a buxom woman with blue breasts.
A cringing dog slinks from the ruins.
It's for him my heart feels woe.
A red dog long in the tooth,
my grandfather with four legs and a tail.
He stretches out under the walnut tree, dreaming
the bone of the moon, a patella of silk,
and jabbering in his sleep as we all do.
When it rains, frogs from the pond stick to my skin:
carnivorous flowers.
I screech once
and my jaw trembles.
The croaking wafts like smoke from a deserted house.
My belly swells and I gurgle.
Once upon a time my grandmother turned into a frog of flesh.
But hate is most ferocious.
Rats stream from my mouth,
squirming, clawing, wriggling with life,
even the red rats.
Their hatred is my lust for biting, hitting, laughing.
The pack—then death, torn limb from limb.

In winter, after the warmth of dream,
I find wolf tracks across the carpet,
forsaken friends who ask for their letters back
journeying through a country of vineyards or through the desert.
They have abandoned their women and children—
who can tempt them now?
Their memory I feel tingling on my lips,
embroidery of spun sugar,
like a grave brimful with quinces.
Allons enfants.
Were the dwarfs feral beasts,
I'd admit they've been swimming inside me
since I threw away my dolls.
They jostle, ricochet in my veins.
In summer, under the dark shade of desire,
I wear a raven's black dress.
It's torn off
only when the sky splits open.
The birds become barbed-wire fences
jabbed into both eyes.
At death's skirts—
worms.
Lacking teeth, lacking desire.
The lamb-queen's heart glitters in my throat
ready to blink back tears, there beside the sparkling lights of the
    house.
For the language of pain has been forbidden us,
the words of blood are too red.

—A.J.S./C.L./R.C.

THE WOMB. LETTERS

One night, when I was about twenty, I returned to my mother's womb.
Here I met some of my half brothers; little Jonah remembered me better than any of the others. To him the world was a deep well. Returning
here was as if I'd died for a night. By what means I entered, I myself
have no idea. Dying inside just a bit, life outside me detached like flayed
skin. In a corner I saw a tall doll. My womb-sister was warm, but my
own body had grown cold. I could not find the small bed with bars,
nor the idiotic rattle toys. Only rich pleasure.

I've made confession to my mother's womb.
She was dead, and, after one powerful wing-beat, an angel.
She still had a single stiff breast
and a hand with six stubby fingers
that grabbed me by the hair to stuff me back inside her belly.
It was a womb like a bed at sunset:
immaculate, soft, with smooth satiny sheets.
Under hyacinths, my brother-grooms waited,
transparent and thrust upright in the air.
It was cold, and from behind bars
the brother-grooms kept petting the rats
thronged together to feast on the flesh of the chosen being.
Shrieks, curses, broken crockery, oh, crazy, crazy mother,
a drunkard for a husband and a thousand sons.
I could have been the thousand-and-first,
except that I already knew the womb was dead.
My brain is a ball of barbed wire.
Monster without a cross, but with a maiden's delicate skin,
the moon has a holy white cornea.
The sons conceived with angels, the father tosses in the trash,
he can't stand them because they aren't savage.
Pink cherubim always buzz around them like flies
depositing sanctified eggs.
Mother, your womb's a nine-story apartment building

and so many sparks wink at the secret feast.
They drink, make love, start over.
Nobody sets forth into the wilderness.
On holidays, the sons stand on balconies and wave flags.
God clangs pots and pans in the kitchen,
guzzles red wine.
Oh, mother, the countless little saints you've conceived!
Some hover high overhead, hiding their face behind their left wing
so as not to be recognized,
while others remain in the white womb and won't come out.
I tempt them in vain with rock candy and women.
Mother pummels the womb-house with her fists.
The massacre of infants is a dead woman—
the sole living woman is the killing of the womb.
Who are you?
You are not The One, yet one of us has sold you
and prayed in the glare of the light, wringing his hands.
I don't know which son, but he seemed a man, a man weeping.

❋

A lotus's scream I bury in my heart,
the size of a child's fist—
and the fist twists in my entrails
reddening both sun and moon.
Within the white bellies they beat with their fists,
pounding my heart.
Their fingers protrude through my ears,
mumbling in a forbidden language of sleep.
Their hands clutch at everything
and tear the immense womb to confetti.
Plug the well, plug the mouth of hell!
No, I won't give birth to shriveled, gummy gods.

Do not bear me before full term.
From the coffin of your womb, eternally blessed blood–duchess,
I see babies rush pell–mell to the slaughterhouse.
Your angelic name beheads me.
Unborn, I rampage, refuse to repent.
Among the coffins you bear in your brain,
only one clatters and clanks.
The warm marsupium of death,
this is what I feel in the night.
You lock me in at the first hint of dusk,
you gently drum on the belly.
Bang! Bang!
I no longer want to bear you,
I don't want to lull you to sleep.
It's raining there in the beyond.
Outside the belly, the drops are soft birds, transparent.
Bang! Bang!
Stop knocking, stranger,
and make for the violet land inside.

—A.J.S. / C.L. / R.C.

THE FOOL OF DELIGHTS

My little concubine,
you have paranoid thighs
and heirloom breasts.
My feet dainty in felt slippers,
I climb on your sweet and delicate bed,
the bed of a desperate doll,
her eyes plucked out, her hair pulled loose.
You heehaw like a donkey,
bray with parted lips rouged blood-red,
and you want me write your biography.
You've planted your violet fingernails in the wall
like hothouse amethysts,
your manikin soul rockets above the sky,
shattering the roof, slamming into the sun.
Hands in my pockets, I watch for
your descent embodied as a gray sparrow,
when my heart will stop beating like a tuneless bell.
Your lotus-white skin frightens me.
I've brought you a marsupium
so you won't go on being half a girl-angel
with wretched, blunt wings,
so for you too there can be a house of salvation,
the cage of spring
where you isolate yourself as deep as blood
and cry out in crystalline cries.
Your bathroom is well stocked
with blades for veins, nooses for the neck.
My hands sweat when I touch them,
when I stroke the golden gleam
so as to consummate an early death.
Cherubim buzz around you and stink,
lead soldiers stand in sullen silence,
the night watchman sees

billowing over the city
the shameless smog of death.
Oh, your pillow is perfumed with Emma Bovary,
with St. Augustine
when he was a dust-covered sinner.
The buttons of your nightgown
are like breasts babbling loudly.
Sleepily they slap my face
to drive me away.
Truly I tell you:
boredom has grown on your forehead
like a leech.
You commit suicide in chiaroscuro.
A jet of holy blood
sets me ablaze from head to foot.
Small astonished fish swim through the fire,
their eyelashes blinking in giddy puzzlement
at the grave in your veins.
I don't want the Greedy Lady to snatch you
with her cracking phalanges,
her dry eyes to spy you
whistling,
I don't want you to spend winter in the madhouse,
where injections tatter your flesh
and a knife skates softly into your blood.
The violet girl sits alone in the room with bars.
For you I festooned myself with this straitjacket,
I go barefoot,
and my guardian angel
has had his wings handcuffed.
My bones knock themselves against the north,
so many owls have shut their bulging eyes!
Terrible is the fog creeping over the dead

like a gigantic slug
that in your anger you want to crush.
It slides along the passage,
glides through the frozen blood,
licks the slick, sliced veins
like a delicate hangman
who wears a tiny cross on a chain around his neck.
I'm writing a biography of you as a hermit.
Your phosphorescent heart sizzles,
your flour-white face gleams madly,
the fragile head I'm afraid to caress.
And the soul with its little milk teeth
nibbles death, crunches death,
beheading the angels who flutter drunkenly,
come to herald your coming.

—A.J.S./C.L./R.C.

EE-HEY-NA!

Ee-Hey-Na! Dance, black panther with ruby lips.
I am lioness of the wheat spikes, invoked as Kore-Persephone,
and I charge you, dance! Shriek wildly, moan in tooth-gnashing
    madness.
Ee-Hey-Na! Twist, spin,
may your spasm ravage earth of her harvest.
Your face cleaves to your bones, your soles slash faster, faster.
Ee-Hey-Na!
Dance! I whip the horses of your honey flesh.
I have bribed burly night watchmen to keep a close eye on you—
Corinth men with curly wine-black beards.
Impassioned demon, savage seeker,
shake yourself, quake the earth herself,
prize out of me the tremors quivering, gathering inside.
Sink yourself in a tempest tangled in hair of octopus,
Salome of smoky Haidos, hey! Whirling she-dervish!
Be my dark ghost and priestess of devouring flanks,
for always the black sun grinds my skin with despair.
Your face, like a clay vessel of olive oil,
my altar anointed with fig wine.
Drink, and I will offer a libation for ascending out of the body.
Don't hold yourself back, become hurricane, typhoon of the steppe,
goad me into a frenzy, devil's she-goat—
arouse both dead and living as one,
that all may dance, pomegranates garlanding our hips.
My bacchante, you're my good-luck charm.
In your dance I felt myself robed in the glory of drunkenness.
On my head I wore horns, a goddess
perfumed with rich spices by worshipful slaves,
my ankles bedizened with tinkling bracelets and trinkets,
my neck unbound from the collar of my husband, god.
I yanked my hairpins out, kicked off my useless sandals,

unbraided my hair, oh crazy ropes
for shinnying up to the brain.
And now I cry aloud, *Ee-Hey-Na!*
My body smokes like a candle; it isn't sick, it flames
when the tongue of your dance lashes, licks my legs.
Ee-Hey-Na! I scream fiercely,
my clothes fluttering like a bat in a storm's forked flash.
The soul of your dancing feet rubbed with savory leads me to the
   sky
and enters though my innards as a whirlwind.
Ee-Hey-Na!
My legs are shriven; they sing in a shivering fountain
when I roll the thyrsus on my head.
Ee-Hey-Na! Bacchante dancing, I'm caught by your hair as in a nest,
my soles bubble with laughter, my feet gush upwards
in this dance with the swish, the slash of scars.
Ee-Hey-Na!

—A.J.S./R.C.

SCHIZO

Cesereanu

KNIFE

Descending to halfway through my days,
I learned what it means to caress with a knife.
I sketched a life map on my skin
and the blood cast polished rubies out of me.
The knife is a glittering animal, my silver house,
an angel to slice mirrors, a tamer.
In heaven a knife-tree grows
with serrated leaves redolent of fall,
and when it withers, shedding its leaves,
the saints shuffle their soles and trickle droplets over the fields.
Oh death, you have stainless-steel wings!
I held the knife against my left breast
and it warmed itself from my heart.
My metallic ventricles would suddenly open—
I'd feel myself dazed by a blow of black light.
Once in the holy times of my youth
I intended to cut off my hair with it and become a nun.
The knife was my father.
He taught me chopping devils to pieces,
sang for me on the cold nights when loneliness slapped my face,
even shouted when I would nibble from always-commonplace death,
I am the life, do not fear.
I loved him sweetly-sourly.
The knife stayed alive in frozen regions of the brain,
a pilgrim through lands without a star.
Those who hear this story will pray for a very long time,
they will call me the executioner's little girl and cry out:
Viper, you have talons like a cross thrust in the ground.
Girl-child, you're heretical from sunrise to sunset!
A knife was the doll I fed and cared for in the pack of childhood,
my sharp life, my cutting mountain,
the same knife I balanced on my head

when I was a bride with white teeth.
From it I would make candles for the dead.
One night I gave birth to knife and he cried like a haunted son,
Mother? Father? A silver tongue licks your forsaken love.
Those who hear this story will mutter for a very long time
in their midnight rooms.
Wearing a white nightgown I kneel and pray,
knife makes his nest in my delirious vertebrae.
I myself am he, his steel, the shiny god.

—*A.J.S./C.L./R.C.*

THE BODY

Woman, you've gone berserk,
your bones break against a wall in the void.
Your heart is split and flickering like a lizard.
I have sold your head and hands to ancient libraries.
May they make your skin into papyrus and a terrifying palimpsest,
so your flesh will be devoured by mental cannibals
who dream of you, whirled about in the astrologer's sleep.
Nothingness has white teeth of ice,
the spine is a cosmic tree with diamonds in decay.
Woman, you are a fever with your innards on the outside,
a she-bear who sleeps in a house of fur and flesh.
Who could retrieve for you the dolls whose heads you pulled off
but whom you fed in your childhood?
Who could have given you that first kiss with little lamb's horns?
Remember, you were a solemn little girl in a coat of mail,
then a girl with hair of flames,
and now the woman of the death's-head moth.
Harpoons have thrust into your neck,
a pink flamingo is wound around your waist like a chastity belt.
At this moment, the crusader who has returned climbs toward to you
swinging his sword over his head as if you were a leprous Jerusalem.
Could you give your body to the starving,
to sip the fruit of your eyes
and your mouth like a little bunny of ivory?
Your body is no skating-rink to crawl on but a site of oblivion
for those who crush you underfoot because you do not want their
    forgiveness.
The fabric of your skin is hard to weave and confusing.
Goggle-eyed, they don't know what to think,
and an eagle's claw like a geyser rakes their warlike chests.
Old jaguars are men.
Immaculate, you watch them as they fall in palaces of viscera,
how they steamroll through libraries of multicolor veins,

how they mix their long nerves.
Their clothing unravels and their skin shrieks.
They carry you to the scaffold to wring your neck,
the flamingo flies away from your waist and weeps for your glory,
the chastity belt retires like an anchorite to a mountain cave.
Your violators will drink in pubs,
utter sweaty smut,
eat their beards full of lichens,
boast like glassy conquistadors.
Carcasses, they want, defiled nuns, monsters of ash.
To them, bodily humiliation is the most terrifying night of love,
they avoid it like the plague-stricken on a desert island.
So much damp fear for the days of debauchery of the flesh.
Ardor is a powerless alphabet
that you master, struggling in crocus season.
But I wanted to speak about touch
just to get rid of it, not to offer praise.
I call the body a humble guillotine,
a white lung with oval nails, Jesuit jade.
Jesuit—this is the secret name for my body.
A single pilgrim awaits my Jesuit,
but this one wanders through deserts and cyanide taigas.
Like a black swan's lover,
I feel his eyes bitter-scented with almond,
the talking armpits, the wavy shoe-soles,
and my Jesuit recites poems with breasts.
The black pilgrim is starry,
he is not a man of death
but the tamer without whip or sugar candy.
The lover is not a rhetor of the skin,
but a prince of camphor who walks on fiery-hot coals.
A wild ninety-nine carat archon,

the lover is a carnivore who cripples the graceful mistresses of the
    mind.
Though his chest is rusted by claws and bile,
nothing can hide his wilderness and realms of denial.
The IV marked him like the sting of a bee,
oh, my holy lover, too many halos have polished you!
My electric Jesuit explodes with a grating roar.
Into a chlorine sea gushing springs pour.
Who am I, man or woman? Neurotic, I swim in a rush
to attach myself to the scales of the rainbow fish.
Dearest lover, monster of an apostle yet unflowered,
I'm the fool of delights and since I was thirty I've been dead.

—A.J.S./C.L./R.C.

THE SOUL

What of the clinking ankle of the heart
or the rapacious territory of the North?
Where is the head and its barren prudish women?
With humility I've always summoned the Inquisitor,
he who eradicated the monsters that bite through veins,
elves, forest dwarfs, as well as nuns in full bloom.
Most of all a morose nun who rejoiced in the dusty war between
    body and soul.
She wore patent-leather boots, a multicolor habit,
and a cross at her hip like a dagger.
She'd always dance around the room of the head,
wheeling in circles like a vulture and praying only much later.
The old Inquisitor had her rip the habit to shreds.
Under it she wore disheveled armor with wolf-bitch scales.
Marijuana, that's the secret name
the Inquisitor calls me whenever I dream in blue.
Gnomes make death signs from the moon.
Marijuana, be the evening's harlequin,
kill the ice-knights lodged between the ribs like a injection of fog.
Off with their heads and hands!
Through the skull's snowy thickets you hear the imperial liturgy,
archangels of flesh knock at the door with their spurs,
the dragon smiles with lips rouged like a woman's,
his widower-spine clattering in a hullabaloo.
Legions of drunken white owls *whoo-whoo-whoo.*
Hey, dragon, through my mouth you reach the heart's orange like a
    woman in August,
you can sleep there, your paws on her tarted-up thighs, begging.
My inner Saint George thrusts her spear into the dragon's bronze
    belly—
am I not a great sinner of secret thoughts,
the ones you keep under your tongue like breath mints
that awake even the dead!

Marijuana, in your head there's a hedgehog buried under the snow,
in your heart, a vixen sleepwalking,
in your body, a she-serpent forever coiled and blind,
and so many other beasts tangled between your ribs,
unstringing necklaces of little bones
beyond the casemate where the man of snow stands sentry,
unmoved in the swelling of the heart's pear.
Marijuana, pray for us.
Listen to the pink flamingo sing.
Autumn churns in the skull as a river of crushed leaves.
Alas, a Sistine chapel of fog hangs in the leather pouch of your
    dreams, bulging full,
alas, for the delirium as black as a bull.
Marijuana, there in the tower of Orion,
in a skeletal shambala under neon,
the soul in ice skates glides free
on a frozen, polka-dotted sea,
and the sea has rooms with indigo curtains
that flutter like angels, swollen and drowned,
the ones you call the brothers lost, never to be found.
The rainbows are warm, their hair finely combed
down to their heels, like maidens lacking kisses.
Zeppelins with arched mustaches
float over pastures and scraped oceans.
You journey to the Rising Sun in a balloon of darkness and light,
where magnolias play hopscotch with splendid feet.
Orion is a kangaroo, hot stars in its pouch,
there the sky makes its bed and sleeps drunk.
Delirium tremens—storms and snowfalls of many colors,
in which God is a ring with agates in clusters.
The Inquisitor says with a red tongue, in Spanish,
Marijuana, I won't break your spine, that your paths may be smooth
    as glass

though the land of the crystalline abyss,
to be the shark of your body, never touched, trickling in the void,
to be your pipe of crippled blood
in the movie of your flesh with daisies where there appear
as a soubrette's small breasts the many sorrows of yesteryear.
The man of snow replies with his tongue of the North Star,
Marijuana, the soul is no more than body—the body hairy, ugly and
    drear.

—A.J.S./C.L./R.C.

Maria Magdalina

For a long time Maria Magdalina has dug into me with a glass shovel
and explored me like an empty tomb.
The king of rats has made his home in my body,
only he will be the bridegroom, the chosen one.
I have no Christ, I will not wash the holy feet of martyrs,
nor will I cry womanly tears.
I lie here waiting and waiting for the spring rains.
My skin is a cold lizard, my body full of plagues.
Industrious little angels busy themselves to purify it
and kill Satan's black flies.
Maria Magdalina, drunk, you have the shakes,
but your body is no more slippery than my hideous soul.
Be a preacher of mystery and deliver me.
For a long time I've sold my soul to madness and perfidious
    beauties—
vultures scour the corpses,
only a baobab of flesh stands under the clouds.
To shout is out of place, to speak not loud enough.
I rave and snarl.
In my heart, a royal archer waits, garlanded in purple.
A slave from nowhere and a lover with no place,
driven from the face of the earth by riotous watchmen,
no wife of thieves or of whirling merchants.
Sailors dreamed me gushing from the moon,
a crazy liquor rushed through my veins.
I was an alchemist's daughter born in a crucible,
they called me Maria Magdalina, not the carnal
but Maria the hidden, the mental.
Sins swarmed under my brow as in an unresurrected corpse,
I had no wings, my head was sundered in two,
I'd grown long claws, the claws of a speaking beast:
my Lord, why has all this been,

unless my body were to surrender on its knees!
It was unravished, like a mountain wilderness
traversed by no untamed beast, and of silver,
for which I atoned like a lavish sinner,
sniffed at by riders, spit at by the covetous.
Why did they lash me, why stone me?
The soul is a field of mortal poppies ablaze with flowers,
where carnivorous goats and Satan leisurely graze.
She-demons bite from your once vaunted glory;
you are in hell now, and haunted.
But hell is in the brain and monsters sing,
despair, it's in vain that your body is holy.
The soul is Barabbas.
The dress of flesh must be torn for good.
The moon stood revealed as black and ulcerous.
Hah! and again *hah!* my sick mouth spews,
only two loves I have, one immortal,
the other a mystery, winged and cruel for spring.
My body doesn't want them, the soul sics them on,
the beast must be defied in the mute dawn.
How can I escape myself, how unmake myself?
My mind's a whore of much too human bone,
the snake and the lamb wedded as one—
the lamb, earthly; horned, the snake.
Maria Magdalina, you are like a gilded mummy,
in my bitter sleep you plummet down, unbound hair wild
and hanging me by my feet,
wringing my neck with delicate greed.
Wash me with a cascade of snow,
spread mud in the veins of young girls,
let them carry sacks rock-heavy with cardinal sins.
I'd exchange my soul for an ordinary body,

even if leprous in its splendor.
What will come of this makes no sense to me though I try,
carnal Magdalina or mental ballerina, Satan, you shall die!

—*A.J.S./C.L./R.C.*

SCHIZO

Come, dread!
Everything will be more alive with you oozing through my veins,
    more fruitful.
As the white lotus flower, the killer, grows from death,
come, dread that's mine, inner woman,
crawl through the tunnel in my brain,
take pity on my common grave,
whip my thin brass ribs
within which I'm immured like a church without wings,
where the grass grows crushed by fire-mules.
I shouted with my thorax, not my mouth,
and purred like a big death cat.
What's inside you, you cannot know.
It's in vain you let yourself be torn apart by the blind man's encrusted
    slates.
I say black as I would have said air, bread, water,
I say death as I would have said suspended life.
I did not stay in the abyss or above it,
but I felt vanishing inside my mouth,
its bitter, stale saliva,
and I found myself mean, without knowing why,
and smothered in faint shrieks.
I thought of the nun's habit,
her second body, so meek,
I squeaked hidden in the night chamber
where nobody could hear me.
I've often lived through dread's lesson
there in the night chamber of my head,
soothing myself with fear's caresses.
With humility, I avow it, power is not holy but tearful.
Never-bright, it rips off the doors and windows,
rakes with thousands of claws from top to bottom.
Alas for those with visible scars, alas for the smiling

and the glorious whose faces it darkened, steaming over them.
I mumbled obediently—could I have belonged to the fire?
Cover me, swallow me, inner woman,
I've never reached the land of angels.
But if ever I were to rise to heaven,
I'd first peek through the keyhole
to see how killers kill and how the killed get killed.
Goodnight, drowned birds and infants with beaks of gold,
farewell, praised mothers and decayed fathers,
sleepily I rock in a glass birdcage.
So much unbridled praise sheltered behind tears,
I could be the ultimate machinery of humility.
Alas, God's dwarfs spy out and trample their monsters.
Nonetheless I was happy I was born,
I would perform tricks with my mind like a white tree,
glad I had a bell around each ankle.
The wolves thundered in the drums, dizzy from absinthe,
I danced stepping over the fire that kept driving nails into me,
and I nibbled on candies like a royal daughter under lock and key.
I am a diver into my head, from the Rising Sun into the Schizoceans.
I think about how far, how deep fresh suffering can reach.
Do you hear, Niniloh? I hear and obey.
It is said that I, Niniloh, once was sold to the devil.
I'd unlock my heart like the door that opens to the secret feast
in a huge sleigh of the body,
I'd glide among the towers and ice butterflies of the inner cities.
Glassy was my woman's way of seeking out madness
and her sharp things that wound.
The fog in its flowering surrounded me like a dazzling dress
in which I could have burned with self-blame.
Fever, the moon is green, my believer's head limps across the sea.
As far as the plague of my thoughts,
it can sputter silently over a candle.

What need do I have for the rabid dog-bites of my mind?
I had been betrothed to fear
and wore its tiny ring on my sixth finger, called the unseen.
Silly, called the un-seer, the voice of a drowned man from the
    Schizoific Ocean called out.
Dementia slowly ascended in the elevator.
A lady of days gone by wrapped in yellowed lace,
she rapped on my forehead with a glass wand.
Girlie, whence did you come, whither are you going?
Hee-hee, thus she'd torment me.
I have come from the hospital of the dark and am going to the
    empty house,
I have come from the North Star and am going to hell.
Don't play with the devils in your blood, Niniloh, they'll make
    you ugly.
Here my Advisor would have said:
how do you know all this,
for you've never partaken of the black core?
Hey, little holy woman,
even if you have your share of lucky dreams,
you cannot rummage through my brain
as through a dower chest—
I threw back the news to the Advisor,
touching her arms I would like to have chopped off forever.
Always dressed in white or in black,
the Advisor saw in me a broken doll
she would have locked up in happy barracks.
Between us was a wall, only a polished wall,
souls were souls and nothing more.
Niniloh, I'd whisper at night inside my mouth,
could you be that downwards path life takes toward death?
Yes, I am betrothed to fear.
Why should I confess for the tears of the tortured,

why does the shroud make me delicate, why do scars give me rest?
The butcher says, a carcass cut in pieces is my life,
the gravedigger says, tender worms consume your life.
I think death built no bridge to this house,
but don't I mistake my expiation?
And if I were to find my own relics years later, displayed in a shrine,
should I not throw my shriveled bones at the crossroads,
like a madman released from the madhouse too soon
who knows what his wounds are murmuring,
that he's the one who once flapped over the world,
tearing open his pelican breast?
Girls with hoops kept drawing the moon split in two.
I entered it at dusk, when the time of stories draws near,
the beaks of tinfoil birds would peck at my mind,
I'd be left with jagged veins, with black words,
and on my lips I knew the same iron symphony:
blood, mayhem, cold.
I always return to the common grave as to my solitary night train.
The tiny lights at the windows are a convoy of the happy dead.
The ancient priests do not pray enough for me,
just as I don't light enough candles for their bewildered photographs.
What's left when I climb aboard the train
is a couple of frantic lunatics' heads that jam into my pockets
full of lymph and other sorry liquids, with no epitaph.
Although embittered, I'd fall asleep at the sound of the blood's sticky
    song.
I'd no proof I was crumbling.
Yet my chalky lament fell over bodies dumped in a heap.
Would Mozart's dog cry for me, too, and enter the story,
would I see, from my stiffened life, how the mourners sprinkled me?
I wasn't to blame for feeling like this long before I died—
the only halo around my head was pitch black.
The Advisor quizzed me about my appetite for despair.

What could I say,
look, I haven't cried for a long time,
I'm happy, even though a viper's tongue keeps licking my thigh.
Suffering was a blind man with twisted skin,
a mole with flowing temples,
but I hadn't the breath of the epileptic of amber.
The way to putrefaction made me nauseous,
the merchants with sticky hands who bargained in the pulpy empire
    of mankind.
I saw myself from high above as in a squashed miniature,
no sweet body, no saved soul remained,
nothing but a big amputation in the void.
My life was an everyday butcher shop
where pork and similar lunatic meats would hang.
Nobody would sit high on a throne of steel,
neither the Ripper, nor the Little Saints, nor the Virgin M,
all had been carted off to the hospital in straitjackets.
If this were a way to be less alive,
if gentle creatures, freezing, could caress
my bright red entrails,
here was the key of my way of being,
red, deepest red.
I felt like losing my mind
when the Advisor and some good-for-nothing wise-guy would say,
You're too cruel, but just delicate enough
so as to stop gnawing at the black sun.
But the black sun was no bringer of darkness,
only the screen that separated my heart from the crowd
so that it could surge ahead.
I could not renounce what was mine like a too warm sister,
that's why I kept saying I, I, I, with a dead man's eye.
I was guilty, I was a leper of myself.
Free as the birds in the sky, as anonymous vagabonds would write,

I laughed until blood gushed from my nose and ears,
the queen's impure blood.
I was the Great Carnivore written in tears.
I'd wear a sword at my waist, or spear or halberd,
and I'd sink in the Schizatlantic Ocean.
There I'd put on the ivy dress,
run through fields of poppies
and see exceeding-joyful Alice ride a toad
to the tea party.
Alice-the-girl could only be seen
when I wore my striped straitjacket.
Then Alice, hunched up in a soap bubble,
shattered against my uncombed hair.
For how long had I been feeling like this, unawares?
The oval hearts were steamy with fear,
the orderlies marched toward Alice to put her in the electric chair
as she clutched a wilted bridal bouquet to her breast.
Come, death, you've sniffed me out,
now kiss me and get thee hence.
I say death but I confess
about a Bible covered with locusts,
an alcoholic stanza or loony paradise.
I would find my bed blown apart
and I ordered myself not to turn the other cheek, too.
Father writhed between limbs,
absinthe sizzled around his mouth,
while he gave birth to me in perfection.
Unsuitable, my parents' marriage bed,
about which I often confessed, shy and ashamed.
Chewing up cherry blossoms in the Schizoidian Ocean
were two vaporous executioners, beheading each other in a frenzy.
Disgusted by suffering,
I uprooted the sun like a rat, glorifying dusk,

I'd had enough cruelty and a fluffy *talion* could be observed on
   my face.
The Advisor set corrugated-paper wings on my shoulders,
I'd attempt to fly, *flap-flap,*
like the door to Heaven, stiff from lack of use.
Then I threw the wings in the world's dumpsters.
In the chlorinated water of my mind, without sight, without hearing,
I'd mix up shells of every different kind and travel over lands
   and seas,
I'd shout until I was hoarse and hurl myself against the aquarium
   glass,
like a female fish with an earthen heart,
and the aquarium seemed a wall like those grown between my ribs.
In the empire I was accursed and had a mistletoe crown on my brow.
Over lands and seas, as I said, I crept
like a desperate galley in the green air.
The orderlies wanted to flay me.
The Bavarian Ludwig with his disheveled hair put finger to forehead,
hee-hee, my dear Ludwig, how many letters I've written to you
with the blood of the dolls,
and to you, mustachioed Friedrich, to Ezra-il-Fabbro and to other
   lead soldiers of the moon,
with half of my head locked in the empty house.
The Great Deaf Man—*da-da-da-DUM*—
Friedrich of the delicious hussar whiskers
or the sleepwalker with his cockeyed hymns,
Ezra-the-Silver borne in a cage before the madding crowd,
and so many others I'm not making up now,
fluffy and terrible.
Dementia, the inner woman,
a soldier she was, too, but made of tin.
For the doll Dementia
I had a change of dresses, shoes, even a bedroom.

At twilight, Dementia would turn into the head nurse
with a starched uniform and the corners of her mouth drawn,
but when she returned to her ways as a doll,
she'd repeat, mincingly, *ma-mà ma-mà*.
The moon lashed my sniveling eye,
what was I pining for without knowing it?
And suffering, howling, grunting!
Dementia, how did I scratch your pinkish skin,
how did the veins arch like bridges?
The abyss touched my soul.
Where on the scale of sins did I belong?
My lover should have heard my stormy blood,
he didn't know that I'm the great love,
not a puny love with only a lead ring.
But the lover believed you a ship haunted by women from
    the drowned.
Alas, alas, go, get thee gone, my love,
could I have whimpered like a pampered lapdog bitch,
wagging my tail by the crippled wall?
Love doesn't mean anything now,
and the mongrel of a great love
inherits only the worst of times.
Not even the saints can resign themselves to a depthless void.
In their insomnia, the uttered words
aren't only the body's mold
but also the root of meaning trailing through the blood,
or the wilted perukes of the brain.
I could remember death as in a body dazzled by sickness,
but I know only a demented formula.
I have a red dress and live inside it as in a monstrous room,
I want to laugh, but I hiss,
I want to walk, but I crawl,
I see in a corner the broken smile of a porcelain doll,

I feel time as a cancer-flower on my brow,
and lazily I foresee a sheep's boredom.
For fluffy happiness I'd live underground,
groping beneath cities and through the brain's cellars.
But there—only silence,
my field of black earth, unlit and empty.
I had three clear things that belonged to this world
and in maidenly order they were
death, love and belief.
Death was the first, a castle of sugar candy.
Love I'd drink with champagne, pulverizing the glass in my teeth.
The pipe of belief dripped for my soul,
it was the only one I wanted to save.
Alice, dear girl, what about killing you
before they strap you in the electric chair!
If only I could die, how I'd enjoy it.
Hee-haw—sing with me, undefeated little donkeys—*hee-haw!*
I come from the North of the North and go back to the empty
    house,
I come from the hospital of darkness and go back to the-devil-
    knows-where.
It rained in the Schizarctic Ocean
and the soul got soaked,
the fish-body hibernated,
the brain made deaf by a saxophone stuffed with coral.
As I sat inside myself like a diaphanous fetus,
born covered by hospital smocks,
fluttering like the layers of bridal gowns.
The grinding of the world is a vain door,
so the anonymous vagabonds would say.
From my hump streamed a disgusting light,
but it was disgust at the overbright and the superfleshy.
Calm down, have pity on yourself, stop trembling!

I made myself calm, but I knew I wouldn't get what I didn't have.
I'd wanted to throw myself from the eighth floor.
I knew I could go *flap-flap* just once,
the pellicle between the angels and me would be so thin
that I might be able to break it.
Sometimes I'd say in a white voice, *flap-flap*,
I'd row with a sailor's knotty arms,
but the ocean I stepped out on with red-hot soles
was lost and forgotten by the Little Saints.
Not a drop of chrism would flow from it upon my neck.
I was frightened by the wall,
but, perhaps, wasn't it soft and tender, wasn't it warm?
A pink flamingo turned to stone on a steppe
I've always wanted in my dream.
Some believed in the wall as in God. Not me!
For me the wall has always been rough and full of cracks,
I did not crush myself against it but protected it with my body.
White vultures would try it with their beaks and then the orderlies
    would shout,
It's not a wall of flesh, white vultures come from nowhere!
Alice would throw the wilted bridal bouquet at them,
but Dementia would let them perch on her shoulder and feed them.
The little donkeys burst into the amphitheatre,
trampling over open Bibles.
Hee-haw, sang the world-famous orderlies,
the syringes jabbed the walls,
the little fire-donkeys danced,
the asylum would rise into the sky like a star,
the exceeding-joyful Alice prophesied:
They have come to break the great padlock.
Exult, throw off your filthy straitjacket
and, in a lightning streak, run for the door!
I cried out, garlands of weeds on my brow,

hee-haw, the crippled little song made us calm.
My hands scraped by loneliness, I caressed the living moon.
Her dark light haunted us.
I'd locked the guards in the clock tower,
the madhouse was gothic, surrounded by tombs of bone,
the donkeys rampaged through the forest after the dervishes,
the delicate and decorated lunatics.
Dementia clapped her hands in soft heresy,
mounted on a headless statue.
Here's the death fiesta in the soul, Niniloh,
olé, thrust the sword into the black bull with its snowy mouth.
Is it your head sprawled in the sand, swinging in the hourglass,
or merely an apparition amputated by the void?
The guards in the clock tower were weeping,
for I kept them locked up in the terrible dark.
Dementia conducted the brass band.
Trumpeters blew toward the heavens and marched in formation.
I ran across the rooftops,
my corrugated-paper wings rustling.
I was the nun, my generation's only cannibal,
while the trumpeters of the band blared,
shrilling into the Great Bearded's left ear, the one with the earring.
The Great Bearded could be master of this world and *that* world
    as one.
His beard reaches down to his feet, half black, half white.
While the donkeys bathed in moonlight swooned with fanciful
    desires,
while Dementia and Alice arrived with tousled hair,
I laughed and cried gleaming for my freedom.
Its bell would toll at dusk as a requiem diluted by silence.
Who waited for me to catch the butterflies on the graves,
for whom could I be the crystal jewel worn at the neck for luck,
who'd dare find out how pitch-smeared and lacy my life was,

who'd know how to caress my death with the skill of the prayerful?
The trumpeters had trilling, forked tongues.
Ludwig, Friedrich, Ezra-the-Silver, the three horsemen of the
    apocalypse,
were budding at nightfall, watered by bright rains,
like winter run wild, without the litany of hoofs.
Oh, brothers of quartz,
how the threefold heart bursts into flames,
the empty tombstones burn,
the fallen angels rave foaming at the mouth,
so many flesh-flowers die in vain,
and nightingales sing inside the beast's veins of incense!
Scaly madmen trample the garden with its iron bars,
as in days of yore ravens grazed in the tooth-grinding snow.
A starry woman, Dementia enters with frozen wolves into the house
    of the head.
Hee-haw.
The bewildered wind scatters the orderlies arisen from the tombs of
    bone.
Straight to me, striding with gigantic steps, comes the Antichrist,
    alone.

APAGE SATANAS!

                                   —A.J.S./C.L./R.C.

Cesereanu

CRUSADER-WOMAN

Cesereanu

CRUSADER-WOMAN

Hell throws open a few windows
on afternoons expert in boredom.
Oh, King of Lead[1] on your Evangelist throne,
the city starts bawling like an invisible child.
Saint Michael[2] plummets crystalline from the sky
as I watch from the bell-ringer's tower
I once wanted to climb,
intending to cheat the city's crucified.
On benches, orange students and old men marry like witches,
while cherubs find they can no longer fly
in this rotting autumn.
Evening's ever-grayer wig
slips off the moon's bald pate,
and all night long the king bows his knees
in this iron Gethsemane
where soldiers on horseback dream of bathing in the blood of stars.
Armor bursts open like a scar,
and the hearts of the ghosts,
the disappointed and the flayed boom like thunder.
The more you will write, Scribe, the more you die.[3]
Broken people, get back from my cruel thought.
You died a long time ago, drifting off to sleep
in hell's pink meadow, between horses and ashes.
But messengers from the north delivered horseshoes,
so you hastened to a war lost before you set forth.
I fly above the city and keep watch
like a colorless angel, like a wall.
The Someş[4], inward Lethe for the guilty,
foresees the faces over which it will shed tears.
You'd believe you're hiding a daimon inside you
if you weren't transparent.
As for me, gloomy cows ruminate inside,

confusing seasons and torment.
This city has nine great churches.[5]
Their saints have congregated to howl
and laugh, to forget why they were conceived.
Let us unravel the socks of penance threadbare from too much wear.
A black mouth swallows the church whole.
Thick-lipped darkness,
fragments of the city catch in your hair.

&

In the alleyway next to the pharmacy museum,
the Beloved[6] faints at my feet.
It was I, the girl of clubs, who had shaken night from his body
and played on his silence, a knife between my teeth,
and who was now dragging him into Saint Michael's,
my tender obsession.
Woman, cursed be thy nature and thy way,
cursed be the rats that squirm out of your mouth
and the garbage of the world you sniff
from the other side of your soul.
On my back I bore the Beloved's body to the foot of the cross.
The church was crowded with people.[7]
From her ears rushed out three demons who hid in the organ pipes.
People sank to their knees, their eyes knives in the air.
Who is the young man fallen at my feet?
Who is the one who wants to set forth into the wilderness
and leave his wife bereft of the house of his body?
This is your chosen one, your son, your brother, your dead.
You won't find anyone more fit,
last night's angels told me.
At long last, the Lover peered between his eyelashes at Jesus
and told me to leave.

People kept flying among the chairs like butterflies,
singing *Ave Maria.*
May it be as you said.

&

A wall of orange brick—
that's how I imagined Jerusalem in Cluj.[8]
I used to pass under the orange nut trees and watch the shriveling
of the reddish hair of the saint killing the dragon.[9]
The beast took sanctuary in the old church
where at midnight you could hear the organ swell.[10]
Tziu, hiu, liu, I was slender in T-shirt and jeans,
a girl wrinkled by rain.
In autumn, the organ plucked much of my hatred out of me
and a little old age.
I wasn't used to insolence,
but still my body did not cause me pain in the darkness.
I sprang from the church,
a lonely woman fed up with suicide.
I babbled in my sleep, I called the city
a crown of thorns on my tender head.
And then for the first time I thought:
Why don't you live here, Jerusalem?
Come to the city of nine great churches, sing with me!
With your peerless voice and my hoarse voice,
we'll whisper, *halleluiah, halleluiah,*
and set out on our journey like an androgyne.

&

Evanescent are the cathedral's days, not like Saint Michael's,
transitory and whitish, with its anemic tower.[11]

I entered longing for the transparent air under its vaults,
but the gift was sandy.
At the stand where you light candles for the living,
a candle was lit for you.
You were behind me, black with fury,
and you did not know that my life was a prayer for your
    transfiguration.
At the place where you light candles for the dead, six candles burned
for six clamorous bodies hissing like mystical snakes.
I don't have seven dead saints.
The cathedral shrieked in its boredom—
empty, a conquered woman, decaying.
The myopic bell-ringer was about to climb the staircase.
The icons buzzed with busyness. I wondered,
Do believers buzz when they kiss them?
Then do they reveal and conceal their desperate hearts?
What do they want from the ultimate cathedral above?
The cleaning lady was busy scrubbing in the dark:
If dust enters even a church, what could this mean?
Woman, don't be so quick to wag your tongue,
This means that angels have entrails and are warm.
Exile remains like a dove
crushed against a stained glass window.

&

Martin and Gheorghe, brother stonemasons
who carved the saint with the dragon,
the king ordered your heads cut off.
And you were brought among the pillars of Saint Michael's,
the huge church.
My Beloved gave me the sign: at the used-book store

quiet Franciscans and plump Dominican friars convened with
Fra Luther's angry crew and a few burned-out crusaders.
Oh, painter Bernardus, you saw them through the spyglass,
then tortured them with your own left hand.
You were compelled by the transparent glassblowers
and the dressmakers with their sharp shears
to put royal lace on their faces and bless them.
In those times Mathias Rex had not yet been born,
he bided his time clutching his sword in his mother's womb
and did battle with angels likewise unborn.
Outside the womb where you are
is the church you cleaved to pieces, Mathias:
Calvaria.[12] It is white and weeps.
There is no beautiful Madonna in the city,
there are many psalmists and archangels of violet marble
but no Gothic virgin.
For this is the city of warriors and torture,
the city of baldachins where princes make love with the crucified.
I could be a mutilated saint in a church in Cluj.
But I am a woman.
A woman among pestilent buildings, beings without ecclesiastical
    robes,
among garbage cans and martyrs in their finery.
Among the trams that devour the church's brain,
it could be Mount of Olives.[13]
You have crown and pelerine,
you linger around the corner of a wall and watch.
You tremble and want to kneel,
your mouth is sad, glittering with little veins,
and your eyelids flutter like wounded butterflies.
I see you and want to touch you,
but my hand enters a strange light, with diaphanous stripes.

Someday you will have been a king of the city
or a martyr with a faint heart,
suicidal knight and abandoned woman.
You are sad and lonely.
I know you're neither Jesus nor the ghost my family longed for.
You're a winged man with bulging eyes.
The light writhes in you like the body of a seduced woman.
My hand is fire, your face biting, but passions won't come.[14]

&

What starts as union and ends as separation?
Thus asked the chroniclers of the old city[15]
during their squabbles with the apothecaries.
They had raised golden hospitals, orphanages,
public baths with the reek of a sewer.
But the churches scratched at one another like call girls
and the altars had turned transparent.
I still can feel the heresy uncoiling like a dead snake.
There were violet preachers, the poor who cringed by the city gates
and licked the wall, servants with bulging eyes who stabbed
cruel knives into the befuddled judge's heart.
The time of plague arrived, despite the city's having no sailors.
Believers drooled with faith
and dug their nails into their own flesh,
so they might feel a less rosy crucifixion.
The tower where they quarantined the sick
had a womb and a shroud trembling with the steeples.
Larvae nibbled from the wall as if from a thirty-day corpse,
a white donkey neighed in the night, its voice heartrending.
Then the bishop's sisters were seen
weeping on the Tailors' Bastion,[16]
and the beggars with scabby wings danced.

Flayed crosses sunken into the abyss,
who are the slippery bastards of our ancestors
that crack within the marble of sleep?
The stench of Cluj aligns itself right here,
a reptilian miasma soured by time,
the perfume of yellowish angels
and of women ravaged by the haunting of the flesh.
These are the bowels of those risen to heaven by force,
the supplicant vomit of the drunkards,
the innocent urine of the orphans,
the latrine of life and death
in which a sticky king inflates only to deflate,
draining out of himself without knowing it.
The shield of the city was three towers,
a barred gate and laurel wreath.
There was a time when Florentines with melancholy hands
carved many a garland.
Then the florid Flemish dreamed of flying pigs.
To no avail, the priests declared them to be dragons.
Birds with transparent ribs perched on rosettes.
Beardless youths ogled their lovers' bosoms,
or perhaps just the stem of low-buttoned boots.
The halberdiers sniffed the reddish wind of war.
Whoever remembers the city's night porters iridescent and
    caterwauling with fear,
because of the moneychangers, the scaly drummers,
the watchmen of hairy lamps,
the moldy light of the outskirts
in which the city appeared a basin with stone bowels.
The night belonged to the statues with cold thighs,
to the bewildered wanderers in a becalmed boat
on Saint Michael's pinnacle, from which
everything, even death, looked foreshortened.

&

What is the traveler who is neither man nor woman?
What is the silence that does not yet exist?
The traveler is the oldest inhabitant of the city.
The silence is memory and ascension.
On Donat Street,[17] the moon left her ghostly trace.
Even the sea surged from behind a viscous tree
and gurgled like a drowned woman.
In the morning, the milkmen sicced their dogs after it,
the garbage men swept it away like a small puddle, unrecognized.
Then all sorts of violet birds waited for the angel of death.
And he arrived, starving and cold.
Lonely, too, the neighbors said in the morning.
I was already asleep and didn't believe in him,
but Donat Street drained the cursed blood from his veins.
I seldom dream of cherubs but I startled awake,
for they had no face or body.
From Marianum,[18] realm of the nuns, I received signs.
I was there to learn among other virgin-divers,
because the sea was agitated by our submissive minds.
Not far away, the midwives' school had been demolished,
and women in labor no longer gave birth to jesuses.
The city, renowned for the deaf mutes and the blind,
mingled slobbering beings with hands like snails.
You were far from me
and a thousand hot and clever things separated us.
We would sit back to back
until you ascended to heaven, moaning,
and I ascended like a knife thrust into the innocent.
Then the moon that I had ripped apart so many times
grinned like an old crone foaming at the mouth.
I don't know whether the city was sounding its death rattle

or we were dreaming in its blue body,
but the kneeling walls shed light
and like a cripple the river kept gasping.
Its brain was silt.

&

Un-lonely-ing is the temple of death.
Saint Michael murmurs for a long time inside you.
Suffocating city, without shadows, without blood,
your body was of lace and your flesh of mirror.
I buried your reversed head between my eyelids.
Behind me I hear rising the mist of death.
The pale, bald star falls
and the aroma of charred angel enters my nostrils.

&

At the city gates Dolorosa falls asleep in the rain.
Nobody would hear her, whether she cries or remains silent.
She clutches a doll in her arms and sees around her only empty
    churches.
On the gray body of the Someş, a drowned man lies dreaming.
Toothless river, you split the city like an axe and you bleat
    debauchery.

&

Now I have to speak about the membranes of faith,
about texts of life and death,
because girls-maidens-women are forbidden to enter these precincts
    of men.
Dixit et salvavi animam meam.[19]

Transparent *ludi-rectores* and shiny masters,
magnificent cantors and shy, lop-eared apprentices
bicker about how to slice reason's aorta.
Cast ye your pearls before swine,[20] the disciple whispers in disgust.
Credo quia absurdum,[21] he says while a beggar slurps the soup of the
    poor.
The saints' anatomy lessons don't get this far,
what is meant to die is as good as dead.
Yes, your soul still remembers.
From the abyss I feel time as it turns purple and enticing.
Magister,[22] the visionary epileptics and superimposed maidens pass by,
we walk slowly, hardly ever atone for our words
and our steps lead us to the cemetery, which is like a dry uterus.
Progenitrix of the dead. Their mother and father.
I am your female disciple and the words make a void of everything
    around.
You hide in the body, you will forget it and accustom yourself to
    death.
Either you burn or you rot.
My prayer is cut short on my lips.
Che tu mi segui, ed io sarò tua guida.[23]

&

I don't know which church is now looming up before us.[24]
The woman who sells candles tells us
that the light snakes in coiled through the stained-glass windows.
Let us tan ourselves in the light of God,
let him hatch us, fatten us,
so that at least once I can feel his fire.
Lord, it is with difficulty that you seep into my soul,
drop by drop.
I can never hear or smell you.

Perhaps you rustle graciously in your old lights,
smelling of clouded wine.
Under the streetlamps, I bump into Luther's daughter,[25]
cheese-like and snowy at the crossroads.
On the other side sits the female centaur with her white croup[26]
where the Sacred Heart languishes.
Mary has a tiara of burning bulbs,
fiat lux for hippies in blue jeans
and pilgrims with a single earring.
Oh, churches that are no one's,
redemption breaks my white eardrums.
Francesca (I call her by her maiden name)
has entrails of gold and is the oldest woman in the city.
Here lies Jesus-the-ugly,
his heart protruding outside his body, fleshy, foamy.
Of sin I did not rid myself, John-John[27] preached so many times.
John is the beloved disciple, but John Sophostomos has the gift,
and you are my chosen one in Cluj, the city of humble piety.
Here I steeled my faith with loneliness.
Here I learned the meaning of mastery over the dead.
I did not fornicate, but I did judge,
I suffered persecution, but I did not persist in repentance,
I was not chosen, I did resist the ways of the creed,
I did not set fear aside, even though I owed that debt.
And I put forth my innocence itself.
Saint Michael's, my beautiful church—
I want to believe but I cannot,
I wanted to believe but I could not,
I would like to believe and I cannot find the power.
My Beloved, I have chosen you straightaway.
I, woman, chose you, man.
The city anointed us
when we entered Saint Michael's for the first time

and a storm arose.
The astonished citizens clapped hands over mouths
because they heard it said, They exist!
From where should I find the compassion to wait?
De profundis clamavi.[28]
Like an amoeba, Jesus had red pseudopodia in every one.

&

Many will forgive.
You are without brilliance,
and I without any gift except for my heaviness of being.
Every day I waste my time in the Gothic square
and the well-fed doves remind me of Venice.[29]
The bench I sit on is a rotten gondola.
Water from the brain's lagoon splashes the king.
Mathias Rex's statue stomps puddles like a child.
The light scratches the stained–glass windows and the crosses break
    apart.
Not a sound can be heard, oh God,
yet something flickers in the old square,
a solitary soul and misplaced pity wheezing.
Clanking from their carcasses,
the citizens do not want to see or hear wonders.
Even if a thin saint passed,
they would think his height just a grimace.
Glory be to the Mother, the Daughter, and the Holy Ghostess,
because if God had been a woman,
those would be the necessary words.
My Catholic and Orthodox halves should not take fright,
Basilio-Niculai[30] should forgive me.
The city stands deserted, its bodies without substance.

The square reminds me of a fabulous sea.
I breathe in the hint of lost ships,
the scent of the sea which has never been again,
our land of killing waters
populated by the drowned, the docile, the violet.
Ulysses, head shaved, eyes bulging,
and Circe, her greenish veins pricked by bracelets,
both float belly-up.
Thus I give birth at noon, near King Mathias.
Great is the sea of the glorious queen of water
and enticing, her soul flows forth.

&

I wandered through the city like a scream ricocheting among the
    walls.
The kid of death kept bleating.
Pain was redeemed through suffering fulfilled,
the inflated senses of the words
crushed against my unwise mouth.
I felt tears for I was a woman, no more than a woman.
The light fell on my shoulders from my hair.
With disgust, with fear, with compassion.
I stood in the utterance of the dangerous feeling.
Oh, hot blood,
haunted in this orphanage of bones that is the body,
my ribs were shrill and my flesh weary.
Flocks of women crashed down from the houses.
The orange lips of the beggar
opened with lustful compassion,
the blind man's eyes like egg whites
gurgled over the tormented face.

I, without the power to know very much about myself,
or about the green heart of the tree murdered by the woodsman's
    saws.

&

Beautiful were the coppery girls,
daughters, sisters, mothers of the body,
on Cluj's streets paved with dry leaves.
It was foggy and smoky,
girls glided by like ships,
their necks like arrows pointing at the moon.
I was a girl-woman on Donat Street,
I knew I did not even have the least power of a saint,
but I was alone like the entrails of my own belly,
once again alone.
I walked along the street in fear, hearing Him cry,
He whose heart was like a soft red church.[31]
The Son of Man cried out and the world grunted its faith in vain.
I climbed to the top of the hill and said to myself,
Death starts here, find out what it is,
who brings it about, and why.
My face turned black with rage.
Country of flies, how the things of death rot inside you,
poor country.

&

Near the Asylum, the cup of the elders,
here lies the church of the man who holds the keys of heaven.[32]
Behind it hangs a headless saint like a flag without a country.
The elders from the asylum search for his head
among useless chamber pots, in gelatinous beds.

These are the frail children of the city,
they want only crusts and a caress,
they're the old dogs and scrawny alley cats,
spitting, fearing their only death.
Their ribs creak, their eyes stare,
their mouth is wrinkled and green.
They kneel.
Forbear, brother gravedigger,
with your shovel of glass and teeth of lime.
I am inside the womb that echoes with emptiness.
With finicky flies on my mouth,
the elders wrap around their hands the viscera of the anonymous.
The gray city was womanly, descending with lust,
shredding the coppery air of touch.
I had fallen from it, my blood gushed away without glory
and flattened against my own heart
as if in a whirling landscape.

&

John Sophostomos, you decreed that I should set forth on a crusade,[33]
as though the city of Cluj had been profaned by my very soul
like a cursed bitch.
You are my mother and my father.
Help me, Lord, to put aside my nature and no longer be a woman.
Behold, I shall lead her that I may make her male.
in order that she also may become a living spirit like you males.[34]
Your crusade will be my crusade,
not of flesh, but of darkness without pride.
And if light is to come to be, it must be empty within.
Woman, in armor and mail, fight for me and have no regret.
This frail thing will make you tough,
you will become nocturnal and ruthless.

Few will understand you or forgive,
but remember, you are the only woman of the crusade.
Your long hair streams from your helmet like a black fishtail.
The horse is your father, the lance, your brother.
At your throat, you wear a cross of buds.
And Jesus is your son, blood of your blood.

&

The beautiful girls of Cluj laugh,
their bodies like honey and dark eyes.
Golden as the ripe days of summer,
tall as bridges in ecstasy over the Someş River.
I floated by, clung to them.
I passed along Donat Street, once thick with magnolia forests,
and headed upriver, the autumn howling through my brain.
The moon fell on Saint Michael's church like a nightcap,
and the square flooded with darkness.
I rode along the banks searching for boats,
then, dizzy, climbed to the Citadel,[35]
by the burning bulbs of the never-sleeping saints.
I returned among buildings that steamed with life and death.
From behind my window I compelled the city to bow to me.
The cathedral glittered and the lilacs' sweetness was deafening.
In the morning, my body was bound like a Chinese woman's foot.
I could hear the bell, God's puffing locomotive,
the forest clung to me like a grieving woman
and hastened to swallow me.
One day I wrote of all these things
on holy Donat Street,
the second tower,
the nineteenth house of kings.

&

I left for the Woman of Tears.[36]
Vertebrae howled and blood fell, ran prostrate on the sand.
There were two male saints and two female saints, dark rings under
　　their eyes.
The musky scent of hashish arose from them.
Death sat in the head's core,
loneliness raved in a priest's cassock.
The Virgin ran away, orphaned,
the female saints laughed with their stone-still bodies.
No one drifted on the sea like a black swan.
Jesus was in the North, among the icebergs,
His hands frozen, his ribs aromatic.
On Mary's forehead, bunches of red flowers with veins.

&

Orange-mouthed dragons served as trams
crawling over the buildings' skulls.
My hair smelled of coal
and around my neck I wore electric garlands.
I loved the tall church as I loved my own father.
Sometimes I fell asleep at its skirts like an ancient nymph.
King Mathias' horse struck me on the shoulder
and all at once, giddy under the sun, I believed I was in Venice,
close to a shrunken palace
where you could hear opera on a victrola.
Biting their moustaches, Mathias' soldiers watched the dark young
　　woman.
The church stabbed me in the heart and ripped me open,
passersby plodded gently on my dismembered body with the
　　placidity of ruminants.

Aromas of times past in yellow satin,
nuns howl in the monasteries of Cluj,
scourging their backs with wet ropes, mutilating themselves,
frail, ugly fiancées of a wanted man now dead.
While Venice vanished like the steam of a failed kiss,
John Sophostomos halted right before me.
Come with me, the crusade is near, your blood is seething.
We will partake of bread and wine
but still we won't become perfect.

&

We sat and wept in The Killer[37]
Champagne flowed from the cask down the throats of the purple
    drinkers,
Serghei the surgeon, Michael the womanizer, and Roland the silvery,
friends of flesh and blood, with hearts blue-purple, without goodness.
Lord, how many golems, how much fear,
we sat in the pub and grew morbid until death had ended.
The crepuscular cartilage got loose in its innocence,
the old chewed and mumbled, and the lovers without honor
    bellowed
there in The Killer.
We borrowed a limousine on credit
and raced through the city at breakneck speed,
roaring drunk, ripped by so much liquor
stinging our brains and our mouths scolding the moon.
Our vertebrae confessed a humiliating love.
A dead bull's red life,
I have a whirlpool in my bones and a rusty sword on my forehead.
They smelled of lost friends, of passionate women,

even though they were men,
they smelled of cyanide and soft hands
that caressed me with hatred.

&

You're neither John Sophostomos nor Jesus,
nor the Lover with his distinct charms.
Cut off my head, tear out my tongue,
my blood races like a colt.
Who are you, all-immaculate one?
I kept writing like an old woman of Cluj,
writing with a knife point and talking on and on
about death. Death.
You were the priest of my dementia,[38]
hot-eyed brother of spring green,
I felt you like a pure object, with wonder.
We breathed incestuously like two bare walls,
you came from the living, I from the dead.[39]
I was happy, I was ugly.
The beautiful girls of Cluj smelled of rich jasmine,
their long legs gibbering like octopuses.
A turbulent mist wafted over the city in a golden cloud.
You were teased in the marsupium of a lucid day,
you were angry, poor wounded carnivore.
I knew you were no pale, anemic prince, but a *poète maudit,*
and our search could turn out to be a lotus.
You had the impatience of quartz like a soldier without a country.
You climbed inside my brain on humid, sour questions:
What is death? Can you see it?
Death was on its way, a young leech, insatiable,

tumbling with fluffy paws.
My death was not your death,
yet our faces both turned dark
and our scream faded out in a mad woman's womb.
You were a kind of unripe, tart lover of mine.
Inside me, Saint Michael's church persisted with its rank smell,
and then I defeated the lonely Brother whom I caressed.
Your blood was sweet and crazed. I adored it.

&

The city—a great bird of sunrise.
With my hair cascading down to my feet, I pant in the hour of heat.
Saint Michael, the imperial church,
stretches its long neck between my breasts.
I cross myself with majestic fingers
and start to write about the yearnings of Cluj.
King Mathias' skull throbs gently.
I drape yellow lace over my face
and in the nights of noon I shatter the muslin ship of my body,
splashing with the quiet scent of my youth.
A bell throbs softly,
the ship, inconstant as a woman, rocks my red heart.
Toward what deserted land, a white Greek island,
toward what dazzling autumn do I go, smoldering?
I dance until death. Dance.
Like a cherub's arrow, Saint Michael's church
spins in my heart with its magnificence.[40]
No blood is flowing, no wound, I'm still writing.

&

I set forth, Magister, on the road with locks and keys, where you
   baptized me.
I felt the crusade in me like a hot loaf of bread.
Don't be like a filly, woman!
Don't gallop to God!
I drank wine like a man,
I raised my lance in the sun,
I clad myself in mail, not in silk or lace,
I cleansed my blood of mud
and set off to trouble the Lord on my quest.
Tremendous was the bellowing of the churches in the city!
But inside me, living emptiness.
I felt the mark of light on my forehead
and the murmur of the frightened heart.
The She-wolf[41] heralded my sins
and my mouth dribbled the drool of fear.
God's stark white made my bones snap.
Do not let madness strike you, Magister whispered,
while the women anxiously touched my horse and spurs.
And so I crossed the sacred hysteria of the city,
beside moonstruck maidens,
beside you, my Master, Lover, mad Brother.
Three men were mine, and Jesus, the fourth, the most secret.
The drunkards from the bars envied my alcoholic pride of death,
the courtesans wanted to tear out locks of my hair.
I was afraid I would be un-lonelied
and hugged the cross to my breast, as a mourning hand.

The beggars, groaning, rushed to bring me good luck,
the knights batted their eyelashes, amazed at such zeal for the crusade.
Then I rushed from the city.
My horse neighed sadly to Jerusalem.

&

Oh, Clujjerusalem,
the vast heart of Jesus broke over my neck,
I drink champagne and yearn to die,
because I'm the only woman on the crusade.
Nobody wants me so much as to cut my head off,
only the women beggars who think I'm a man
fervently lick my soles.
Lord, how I looked for you
so that I wouldn't be a woman,
so that, smiling, you'd invite me to battle,
you'd put me to the proof.
My love is heavy and strong
and needs no tears.
I want to eat from your red heart,
I want to drink your blood—and drunk, to cheer, *Ave!*
John Sophostomos is far away,
the Beloved in perfumed sleep,
and the mad Brother has abandoned me.
Alone, I'm here for my wedding with you.
Fear pounds at my temples,
squeaks like a magic mouse
that gnaws on your scratched and piercing heart.

&

Trams screech in my brain like glass beads.
Calvaria sits on the conical peak, its eyes aglow
at its churchly flesh never caressed by a man.
Oh, kind Calvaria, how the glances of passersby flow
over your mangled womb.
I climb nearby Golgotha with its tall grass,
near the bell tower that creaks.
The saints' carillon chimes deafeningly,
booms in my shy eardrums.
Then boredom heats up
like a corpulent courtesan of the Lord.

&

You abandoned me, tender Brother.[42]
The deliria, not deliriums, dispersed,
when a macabre head haunted the streets and swallowed the void.
My madness stayed old without you,
with the flaccid skin of forbidden thought.
I'd hear you cry at night: aside from a minor dementia,
we both shared a seraphic incest,
born from the caresses of those fallen in vain.
There were afternoons thrilling in sweet blasphemies,
in the conquerors' soft heresies.
You left for tooth-grinding distances,
in vain we waited for you in Jerusalem.
I knew you'd be brought back dead and forever lonely.

With violet claws like a drowning man's, your veins pitch-black,
waiting insane for your nerves to tingle,
to pick nostalgia from your bones,
cursing kings, enraged at the dead for no reason,
and the complacent exterminators all in one place,
howling furiously because of the quiet tears of others.
At dusk you'll be strapped in the electric chair,
your dumb viscera will dream sweet dreams,
the wheel of your heart will pump less blood,
and, oh, how painlessly it will stop the soul's machinery
on which rebel sleepwalkers have already been gnawing,
craving a gram of silver from you.

&

I listened to pregnant women in their birth pangs,
I listened to saints in their slumber.[43]
I tore out hearts and souls,
the body held tight by girths was not a lamb, and the colt was velvet.
I wore a bow in my hair, no cross at my neck.
Even though a small, timid angel was near,
I turned my back on him.
So much cruelty came from the sun, gushed out of the trees,
climbed my neck and stopped at my forehead.
It was said I wore a mistletoe crown.
That my lovers tortured me for my pleasure.
Luminous anger consumed me.
Dissolute pendulum clocks struck the hours of my chest,
I had a spine of brimstone, I had three breasts each betrothed,
I passed by at dusk sleepily, my hair of tar.
With his own priceless flesh, Jesus fed the lions' den.
Peerless was the pain,
Peerless were the drops of blood like perfect cherries.

I felt a cross of honey in my mouth.
It could be Jesus in Mary's womb,
kicking his little legs of light.
Fingers singed like insects in the candle flame,
my heart turned tender while champing because of my young blood.
The moon split my forehead and fled naked from the house.

&

You were lamenting, Crusader-Woman, near a grave of shadow,[44]
the city would banish you ever farther eastward.
Jerusalemcluj was a knife of soft gold.
Your cloak would swell with sadness like a whale.
Here lived the homunculi of rosy saints.
You poured carafes of wine on my hair and neck,
mercifully killing the charismatic sinners.
The invertebrates' church rises near you
and toxic darkness buffets your eardrums.
Oh, too little Crusader-Woman,
your lance creaked, stuck upon your thigh,
and the horse kicked Jerusalem with its four misty hooves.
Sinners wanted to lynch you, girl,
the odor of death was borne everywhere by stags with brass muzzles.
They accused you of being a holy grave-robber.
My Brother got killed in his sleep like a dog,
the Beloved awaits a sign without blood.
Diaphanously, Magister stood in your Jesus-saturated soul.
At Jerusalemcluj, heralds on horseback cried out,
a man with a woman's body wanted to cleave asunder
the ruby Sacred Heart.
The odor of blood cheered you up,
again you felt the crusade inside you like a hot loaf of bread,
you breathed through your shining bronchi, as high as the moon.

No one was astonished by your silky hair cascading down to
    your feet
or your violet eyebrows.
You believed the Sacred Heart was a carnivorous plant,
a mosaic of mystic scents or a scaly-red lotus.
The cathedral was surrounded by barbed wire,
the guards watched you with soft, swollen eyes,
your tongue hung heavy in your mouth, but gold,
pregnant women with bulging eyes circled like vultures,
and the mountain burned to coal.

&

I glue the dead Brother's head on my own neck,
so I can feel his black blood embracing me black.
On their ankles crusaders wear silver bracelets
that can be unfastened only by nuns.
The executioner retires to his night chamber
where his mistress awaits him.
In the gardens, beasts howl,
the air inside shreds the burning candles
like the headless bodies of men.
The Brother sits in fire.
With my three sharp hands I chop him to mincemeat,
he is flesh of my flesh enameled
by the broken sound of the bells.
In the uniform of Jesus,
Magister signals me it's a feast day.
The crosses have their veins sliced and white.
The Beloved shows up like an alluring crypt
in which I could always die.
The sinners rattle like precipices,
do I jump, do I not jump!

At the city gate, the passionate jostle to try to touch me.
Oh, Clujjerusalem, your red love, like a cup
in which you've collected the frozen blood for so many centuries,
has turned upside-down.

&

I used to stroll under the city's streetlamps,
the russet hair of Venice fluttering,
I smelled the squeamish martyrdom of a few dusty saints
and, that decadent spring, drank wine alone.
I wanted to see John Sophostomos, as thin as a lightning bolt,
the Wise Man rustling together a blitz-crusade,
and I was halleluiah-ing.
Male nurses issued forth from the morgue as from a season
and told me it was snowing in Jerusalem;
they stared dumbfounded
and told me that Jesus had not lived in that land.
I pricked up my nostrils, smelled the dead smoke, and stood
    in bitterness.
John Sophostomos, I was a reckless girl and you turned me into
    Crusader-Woman.
I did not search for anyone's corpse and I did not quest after the
    Sacred Heart.
I felt sick of red,
of the dreadful blood with orange threads.
Your church was juicy.
All around, the crippled had dizzy bowels,
the hungry saw Mary as a succulent woman with marzipan breasts
and ate her. Drank her. No one slapped them across the face.
It is the injected hands of the crucified that I see in every dream,
their white muzzle gnashing like a clam that had lost its wits.
The solitary one has died and will not rise again.

Magister, my head shrinks into a broken shell
and my blood flows no more.
With your whip, you trained me as a Crusader-Woman, you made
    me what I am.
Teresa of Avila sits trustingly in her chains and moans.
I feel pity for her, because she has neither angel nor star.

&

How I beheaded myself, old Innocent!
Your beard fell hissing on my back
and the cross lifted my chest like a trapdoor.
You died far away from the Crusader-Woman.
You weren't to see the electric land where I was born,
or to bandage my rose-blue feet
on the road to Jerusalem.
Let me be Mary, you Jesus:
you're my grave of memory, I'm your living grave.
And let Cluj be chopped to bits by the knives of the lost cities
where you could not be born a seraph,
where you died without splendor.
My guilt is hot blood drop by drop. Living blood.
Take the cup and collect it.
Mad wolf, driven away by she-wolves devoid of light,
it took me so much time to be born Mary,
it took me so much time to find you, Jesus.

&

I returned from the citadel, emerging from the red womb.
Once I had been the Woman-Scribe.
With the last drops of wine, I rubbed my numb eyelids.
The inhabitants had hidden inside the walls,

the beggars buried themselves of their own free will.
At the foot of Saint Michael's stood Magister
with his sad core of holiness.
My Beloved prayed for me feverishly.
Crazed, I sifted my Brother's ashes over the nine churches.
Heavy was my soul and the suit of silver mail,
the lance made me so dizzy I wanted to disembowel myself.
The beautiful girls of the city had lost their liveliness.
The streets croaked, white ravens everywhere.
I returned from the crusade lazy as a snail's daughter.
Hey, soldier, woman of embers,
you didn't wear death like a black flower on your helmet.
The sun's skins were torn from their hinges, its spine was phosphor.
A secret feast plunged through a broken stained-glass window
in Saint Michael's.
I knelt beside the father church.
Behold, I shall lead her that I may make her male.
in order that she also may become a living spirit like you males.[45]
Like you I will never immure myself.
Old, dry, harsh was my heart,
terrible was my torment, slithery men.
Jerusalemcluj shunned me as one of the century's raving lunatics.

&

Iron. My saliva made my mouth cold,
I collect my blood in frozen cubes. Frozen.
I feel my cloak writhing and I scream from all my bowels.
The cry echoes from every roof,
winds around the deserted houses, stabs itself into myself.
A sharp-fanged animal waits for me at the She-wolf,
for the day of tearing to pieces.
All winter, men with long hair and beards died,

parents and soldiers say that we saw
only a phantom-death, just a death killed in the snow.
I'm still warm.
The vapors of life enfold the square
in the soft heat of the trembling body.
I take courage and hurl myself into space from Saint Michael's tower.
Oh, iron cherub, I hear your tameless flutter in the distance
as my head smashes on the pavement
like a glass without light.
Let not this cup pass me.[46]

—A.J.S./M.M./R.C.

A Key to the Poem "Crusader-Woman"
(Wandering in Jerusalemcluj or Clujjerusalem)

1. The entire poem is a quest wandering among the churches of Cluj, but the space of the convergence of memories is Liberty Square, under the patronage of the equestrian statue of King Mathias. He is not necessarily a guide, but an emblematic character who incarnates the Middle Ages.

2. The obsessions of the poem, namely the passage of time and the inexorability of death, together with the quest for God (in its extremes: denial and crusade), have as their material manifestation Saint Michael's Church, which rises in the center of the city.

3. The first living character of the poem is the Woman-Scribe. Ageless, traveling through the centuries. She will turn into the Crusader-Woman at mid-poem.

4. The Someş becomes a mythic river as the real Nile had been in ancient days, or the imaginary Styx. It is sort of a *raisonneur* of the city.

5. The city has many more churches, but nine is the number of churches that the Crusader-Woman will happen upon in her peregrinations.

6. The second living character is the Beloved. He will be the initiator into death, having above all the characteristics of a hermit.

7. Saint Michael's Catholic Church is the omphalos of both the city and the poem. Built between 1350–1480, tall, gray, thin. It can also be said to be the Gothic Ballerina.

8. The city has two faces: the crepuscular and decadent face is that of Venice, the holy face that of the Jerusalem aspired to by the crusaders.

9. The statue of Saint George (Gheorghe) killing the dragon, cast in 1373 by the brothers Martin and Gheorghe. The dragon is no bigger than a lamb.

10. The Minorite (Franciscan) or the Reformed Church built between 1487–1516. Deaf, with orange lips.

11. The Assumption of the Virgin Orthodox Cathedral, built between 1923–1933. Fat, of a buttery color, and fully matriarchal.

12. Calvaria, the remains of a Benedictine abbey from the 11th century, then a royal monastery until 1556. An amnesiac church, eager to forget its past.

13. It is through Jerusalemcluj that the road of Jesus passed.

14. Unlike Martin, George (Gheorghe), and Bernardus, this ambiguous character is a ghost. Nevertheless, if I were to look for an identity for him, it

would be Innocent, exiled and wandering through foreign lands. His figure appears as an emblem of a Cluj protesting but defeated.

15. It is here that the poem begins with the evocation of the medieval, half-heretical city, where wretchedness is mixed with faith, the diaphanous and refined with the swinish.

16. The Tailors' Bastion was built at the beginning of the 15th century at the southeast entrance of the city. Nobody can go up to it anymore.

17. The street where the Woman-Scribe once lived and where the Crusader-Woman wanders on the road to Jerusalem.

18. The Faculty of Letters of the University of Cluj was formerly a convent-college. It smells like an old spinster.

19. *Ezekiel* 3:19-21.

20. *The Gospel According to Matthew* 7:6. But the other way around.

21. The paradox is Tertullian's. The Crusader-Woman believes in his words. The initial variant was *Credibile est quia ineptum est.*

22. The third living character is Magister. He will initiate the Woman-Scribe, transforming her into the Crusader-Woman. Magister is not a fanatic, and the Crusader-Woman will be his act of faith.

23. Dante, *Inferno* 1.113.

24. The Church of the Transfiguration was built by the Franciscans between 1775–1779. Nicknamed the Despairing. It was, and still is, the Greek Catholic cathedral.

25. The Lutheran Church was built between 1816–1829, in late baroque style. Fleshy as a butcher's wife.

26. The Franciscan Church was raised on the foundation of a pagan temple. Before the 13th century, it was a Roman basilica. It belonged, in turn, to the Dominicans and Franciscans. Also called the Golden Gallows.

27. The Magister's name, in his disciples' circle, is John Sophostomos, i.e., Wise-Mouth. John-John, his nickname, connects him to the Baptist and the Evangelist.

28. *Psalms* 130.1. The Psalm of Repentance.

29. The Venetian quality of Cluj, its crepuscular and decadent side. Liberty Square becomes Piazza San Marco without its wonders, and the image of the lagoon is an intentional hallucination. The only truly Venetian vestige is olfactory: the smell of the lost ships. The master of this fever is King Mathias.

30. My grandfathers were both priests: my paternal grandfather from the north, the Greek Catholic Basilio, and my maternal grandfather from the

south, the Orthodox Niculai. They were equally above argument and discussion.

31. The Crusader-Woman's first perception of Jesus in her childhood.

32. Saint Peter's Church, constructed in the 15th century in Roman style and reconstructed in Neo-Gothic style in the 19th century. Also called Mother of the Wounded.

33. Setting forth on a crusade as a ritual of growing up, the Crusader-Woman will besiege and conquer exactly the city she left from: the perverted Cluj.

34. *The Gospel of Thomas* 114.

35. The Citadel was built in 1716 as lodgings for the imperial garrison. It collapses slightly more day by day.

36. The Piarist Church where, according to twenty-eight eyewitnesses, the Virgin's icon wept for two weeks in February 1699. Nicknamed the Weeping.

37. The Killer pub does not exist in Cluj but on the outskirts of another city. The old Three Lice and Arizona, or the Fainting Bitch, to be found somewhere in a lost village, have something of The Killer.

38. The fourth living character is the Brother. He initiates his sister (the Crusader-Woman) into sour madness.

39. From a poem by Tudor Arghezi, the famous Romanian poet, a little bit modified.

40. Paraphrased from the sensations of Teresa of Avila in ecstasy.

41. The Statue of the She-wolf. Also called the Dour.

42. The mad Brother's flight before the holy city resulted in his killing, executed by the crusaders.

43. Flashes from the Crusader-Woman's adolescence.

44. The entrance of the Crusader-Woman in Jerusalemcluj or Clujjerusalem and the punishment of the sinners.

45. Again *The Gospel of Thomas* 114.

46. *The Gospel According to Matthew* 26:39, 42; *Mark* 14:36; *Luke* 22:42. But the other way around.

—*A.J.S./M.M./R.C.*

By a Tiger Writ: An Afterword

She is a prose writer and an essayist, a professor of complit & polisci at the University of Cluj, a cultural animatrix, a historian of violence and the gulag, and, to propose this (pilgr)image to the *factotum,* a formidable poet who said things no one else had the guts or flair to say in Romanian lit. She is not chained to Romanian: she's free in it; she writes in English like a native (see her "Letter to American Poets" in this volume) and in Spanish like a lover. A few months before JFK was caught in the magic bullet's dance of death, she was born in Transylvania (the slow land, not Dracula's), and was left to wander the earth dressed stylishly to the bone. This would do for the infomaniac bent on canned knowledge.

Hey! Open the can and Ruxandra Cesereanu will jump out! She is the smile bearer to the unsuspecting, the devotee to the passerby, the quick one to the dead-on commoner. But: Rux is the witch whose pointy hat hides snakes, apples, and a fragrant breeze that's the parachute of the soul forgotten behind in the messy fall from paradise. She undulates on the page's seas. Her lines are feline, not straight. Let the kitty out at night and she'll graze stars and come back a tiger. These lines' wavy shapes link A & B in passing through the cosmetic survival of the life they barely had. Her lines shoot at you, candid reader, to get—and get you—somewhere not here, for "here" is missed, shot through with bullets. "Safe" is for the weak. Yet, as no-thing and -body is safe—mom's womb, blown open to material threats, forgot how to protect—these lines are for the strong. *En poétesse,* Rux is a tiger.

And the jungle is rich: there, bodies are left undevoured by souls; eyeless, toxic demons roam free beyond the palm trees of freedom; the other demons' infrared eyes pierce manneristically the entrails of whatever; virginity never was. Through the Maelstrom of this tidal cornucopia, the fascinating tiger's skin calls to be seen. A moment after your eye sees it, the other one glimpses the lateness of warnings. The wavy tiger's stripes threaten with urgency. You, candid reader, must face it—it, the defacing tiger skin! For you're now on shaky ground, on the mapquake's hash that Aristotle the pharmacist holds in a jar labeled "energeia." Between her passing selves—the lion and the panther—you ain't got the leisure to be A or B. As soon as you see the tiger writ, you are it.

I saw Rux's writ while drifting around my archipelago (the sirens were safe, the Cyclopes were meek, old Scylla was weeping, her twin had a leak, I was bored). The tiger's writ gave the Baudelaire within me a jolt: eternity's dumpy breath sank somewhere. The sail got set to get me drunk. I got ready for the fight. (The heavens? Who cares? Who cares, cares, but Rux doesn't, and neither does this felinized I).[1]

Proust's madeleine was the Eucharist to many a modern; Rux dips it as a tinge of memory in a sea of remembrance. In Spanish, she writes that lilies brought her the first smell; in Romanian, *the stench of the* Venetian *lagoon was my first Proustian madeleine, which pushed me to dig in my memory for a sensation a few thousand years old—whose being I couldn't fathom up until today* (Venice with Violet Veins. Letters of a Courtesan).

While her lilies are heavy with scents of Caribbean cloak and danger, Venice has stunk for millennia to buffer the turf between death and man. Death surrounds Rux's madeleines like an aura that squeezes the monotonous out of a woman's pathway. A primal scene: no second thoughts; depth pure. It takes a diva to dive to marianic depths and *keep in our lungs the breath of madness.* So does she, and finds on the seabed a knife that, *like death's free fish,* points the way to no exit: *Death journeys like a ship of fluff up to the bride's heart, / the traces of the body rosily disappear, / where's mother, where's father, / where their agony wedding?* ("The Bride's Heart"). Then, *descending in the middle of life*'s way, as she *was drawing* that *life's map on skin* with the knife, there appears *Father Dostoevsky* with *a blue brain.* One wouldn't dream of the merely oneiric: here this patchwork is becoming as surreal as are dream catchers and dream tigers. The descent is not straight: it's wavy blue and head-rush sharp.

Sometimes, as it relentlessly happens in the long poem "Crusader-Woman" that gives this book its title, that descent comes to a boil in the alchemic crucible of reversals. Here, the Transylvanian capital, Cluj, which turns around the omphalic Saint Michael's Cathedral ("from [whose pinnacle] / everything, even death, looked foreshortened"), turns out to become the fabulous city that it is—a foremost station of the Passion's course: Clujjerusalem. The beasts out East have since the beginning cried out for crucifixions; Rux, the Woman-Scribe become Crusader-Woman, tends her cross between Venice and Jerusalem. The geographies of this crushing poem map out a Cluj of nine churches smelling of blood, forgetfulness or cinders, through which the Crusader-Woman wanders and marches from everywhere through nowhere and beyond.

From the heads-and-tails game of "where not to go?/where to go?" came about Rux's most telling volume to date, *Schizoidian Ocean,* to carve nerves and monadiamonds out of life's mishmash. The center of its anatomy is the heart, which *swollen with red, was shivering, / like a girl facing a jealous killer.* Like a crane, the heart's throbbing lifts the shield of memory, the bronze of which, in turn, tolls for the agent of danger: *I was recalling that one, who could live only axe in hand, / likewise, myself with an axe in my head.* The sentimentalism of binaries apart, her images split along the axe's axis, ready to face the labyrinth they are about to engender, Venice perhaps. She, *barefoot, steps over the black fire* surrounded by her memory; but *always turning speechless by crime and punishment, / life's signs are cold* ("Tristana"). That crime called "soul" is not to be punished—this would be the trick of guilt, and guilt has no other language than Langue—but traded: "I'd exchange my soul for an ordinary body, / even if leprous in its splendor" ("Maria Magdalina," found in the "Schizo" section of this book). Every-thing is a body whose soul leads to nothing; "the soul is no more than body—the body hairy, ugly and drear" ("The Soul," also in the same section).

In *Kore-Persephone,* a volume solar in its first half, like the Greece it invokes, the poetess is now a lioness, yet a woman in love with the godly dolphin Korin, after having been a black panther, *some time in the past, / when the tunnel in my head was a city erected in the jungle / by a carnivorous, lengthy woman* ("The Black Panther"). Love jumps beyond itself and light, though. *One day I entered in the cave of my body / aloof and scared stiff* ("The Cave"). Kore-Persephone finally appears in terrifying splendor, a woman-goddess given to the darkness below, speaking in that first person that only the lyre knows how to foreground and help endure: *Next door from Athens' clamor / lies the suburb of sea divers, Sepolya City, / Dark haired youths with branch-like locks and bodies in the midst of needy youth. / As a goddess of the muddy chasms, / I saw them often contort in Sunion's red earth, / as if they were Haidos' faithful followers* who would become, for half of each year, the goddess' attendants; they are drinking and fighting and making love to each other and she (I) would like to peep through the keyhole to their manly twists and swirls, but bearded Haidos prohibits her from doing so. *They scratched graffiti on the walls, / those Achilleses and Ajaxes perverted by the damned century* who were giving her baths until *Haidos-tasting-like-saffron burst in* ("Sepolya City"). Offended by these young samurai who'd offer no sacrifices to her, she takes revenge; one of them is pushed to dive off a cliff into the sea but, as she had had him entangled in a net of ivy, he crashes against a rock, *a massacre it was of young and manly flesh. I am both a girl and a woman, but I could be a man as well,* she shouts at them *rattling the snakes in her hair,* and *could hurl you into the pitch black abyss.* Rux's epic breath, the over–Sapphic length of her stark lines, fathom revenge in even darker tones (for wherever the sun shines brighter, there looms a danger darker, which transcends imagination into the land of unrequited fear).

"Come, dread," the invocation that triggers "Schizo," the longest and concluding poem of the section of *Crusader-Woman* that borrows its name (originally published in *Schizoidian Ocean*), is as hopelessly hopeful as Marlowe's Faust's "Veni, veni Mephostophile!" Rux's fear, though, is an "inner woman" she summons to "crawl through the tunnel in my brain" (her later avatar will be called Dementia; an earlier one, Niniloh) and she, "a diver into my head, from the Rising Sun into the Schizoceans" with "bright red entrails" where "My life was an everyday butcher shop," would keep on going. The madness of being born is that of splitting ceaselessly (her parents: "Chewing up cherry blossoms in the Schizoidian Ocean / … two vaporous executioners, beheading each other in a frenzy") and of having to dwell in the nuthouse of Being— "the asylum would rise into the sky like a star"—where the clustering mad(wo)men gesture away: "My hands scraped by loneliness, I caressed the living moon." The intense imagery waterfalls in the grand finale of this Revelation, where "the three horsemen of the apocalypse, / were budding at nightfall, watered by bright rains," and "the fallen angels rave foaming at the mouth, / so many flesh-flowers die in vain…. / Scaly madmen trample the garden with its iron bars, / as in days of yore ravens grazed in the tooth-grinding snow. / A starry woman, Dementia enters with frozen wolves into the house of the head. / ... Straight to me, striding with gigantic steps, comes the Antichrist, alone. // APAGE SATANAS!"

Crescendo after crescendon't, Rux's feline lines turn into tsunami crests and their invaginated abysses. These lines once were contouring an Ottoman empire of senses to get the better of provincial trances and numbness. Now they're heightened to have sensation overwhelm sensation and create, through the meanders of sense, a cutting sensuousness assembled in an Argus like haREM: the hell of it all next door from hell. In the multiplicity of these witchcrafts, what does the unrhymed rhyme with? In major tones, Rux shows through flickers the tiger writ inscribed on her skin. She meanders with intensity. She is uncanny Slalomé. She's there for you, for only the strong deserve a good beheading on the *blinding guillotine.*

Călin-Andrei Mihăilescu

Note
[1] You will not find here an interpretation—that dubiously flat and certainly postmortem exercise that would better be called "postpretation." Instead, I'll ensconce a dialogic co-presence with Rux's tiger writ. Her lines that I translate appear in italics; mine in Roman; lines from poems in this book in quotation marks.

Călin-Andrei Mihăilescu is a tetralingual writer and a Professor of Comparative Literature, Critical Theory, and Spanish at the University of Western Ontario in London, Canada. His recent publications include seven books in Romanian.

Ruxandra Cesereanu has firmly established herself as one of the most important and exciting Romanian writers of today. Born in 1963 in the city of Cluj-Napoca, the traditional cultural center located at the heart of the region of Transylvania, Cesereanu began publishing poetry in literary reviews in 1981, but her first book, a short novel, *Voyage through the Looking-Glasses,* came out only in 1989, the year Romanian communism was overthrown. She has published nine books of poetry, five books of fiction including two novels, and significant essays on the Romanian gulag and political torture. She lives and works in Cluj, where she is an editor at the cultural magazine *Steaua* (*The Star*) and Professor at the Faculty of Letters (Department of Comparative Literature) at the Babeş-Bolyai University. Cesereanu's collections of poetry include *Garden of Delights* and *Live Zone* (both 1993), *Fall Over the City* (1994), which won the Poetry Prize of the Cluj Writers' Association, *Schizoidian Ocean* (1998, 2006), *Crusader-Woman* (1999, an anthology), *Venice with Violet Veins. Letters of a Courtesan* (2002), and *Kore-Persephone* (2004), which also won the Cluj Writers' Association Poetry Prize. Her prose works include *Tricephalos* (2002, a novel), *Nebulon* (2005, short stories), and *Birth of Liquid Desires* (2007, experimental prose). In 2007, she also published *Forgiven Submarine,* a book of poetry written collaboratively with Andrei Codrescu. It will be published in English in 2009. Her first book of poems in English, *Schizoid Ocean,* was published by esf Publishers, Rochester, in 1997. *Lunacies,* translated by Cesereanu with Adam J. Sorkin, came out from Spuyten Duyvil/Meeting Eyes Bindery, New York, in 2004.

Adam J. Sorkin's recent volumes of translation include Magda Cârneci's *Chaosmos,* translated with Cârneci (White Pine Press), Mihai Ursachi's *The March to the Stars* (Vinea Press), and Mariana Marin's *Paper Children,* done with various collaborators (Ugly Duckling Presse), all published in 2006. Other books include Radu Andriescu's *The Catalan Within,* translated with the poet (Longleaf Press, 2007). His version of Marin Sorescu's *The Bridge,* with Lidia Vianu (Bloodaxe Books, 2004),was awarded the 2005 Corneliu M. Popescu Prize for European Poetry Translation of The Poetry Society, London. Sorkin is Distinguished Professor of English at Penn State Brandywine.

Claudia Litvinchievici is a graduate of the English-German department at Babeş-Bolyai University of Cluj-Napoca, Romania. Litvinchievici is the translator of Ruxandra Cesereanu's book, *Schizoid Ocean.* She is co-translator of five poems in *Lunacies* by Ruxandra Cesereanu (New York: Spuyten Duyvil/Meeting Eyes Bindery imprint, 2004).

Madalina Mudure has a BA in English and German from the Babeş-Bolyai University in Cluj-Napoca, Romania. Currently an MA student in American Studies at the University of Amsterdam, Mudure has read papers at national and international conferences and is interested in women's issues.

TITLES FROM BLACK WIDOW PRESS

TRANSLATION SERIES

Chanson Dada: Selected Poems by Tristan Tzara
Translated with an introduction and essay by Lee Harwood.

Approximate Man & Other Writings by Tristan Tzara
Translated and edited by Mary Ann Caws.

Poems of André Breton: A Bilingual Anthology
Translated with essays by Jean-Pierre Cauvin and Mary Ann Caws.

Last Love Poems of Paul Eluard
Translated with an essay by Marilyn Kallet.

Capital of Pain by Paul Eluard
Translated by Mary Ann Caws, Patricia Terry, and Nancy Kline.

Love, Poetry (L'amour la poésie) by Paul Eluard
Translated with an essay by Stuart Kendall.

The Sea & Other Poems by Guillevic
Translated by Patricia Terry. Introduction by Monique Chefdor.

Essential Poems & Writings of Robert Desnos: A Bilingual Anthology
Edited with an introduction and essay by Mary Ann Caws.

Essential Poems & Writings of Joyce Mansour: A Bilingual Anthology
Translated with an introduction by Serge Gavronsky.

Eyeseas (Les Ziaux) by Raymond Queneau *(Forthcoming)*
Translated with an introduction by Daniela Hurezanu & Stephen Kessler.

Poems of A. O. Barnabooth by Valery Larbaud *(Forthcoming)*
Translated by Ron Padgett and Bill Zavatsky.

Art Poétique by Guillevic *(Forthcoming)*
Translated by Maureen Smith.

Furor and Mystery & Other Writings by René Char *(Forthcoming)*
Edited and translated by Mary Ann Caws and Nancy Kline.

Inventor of Love by Gherasim Luca *(Forthcoming)*
Translated by Julian and Laura Semilian. Introduction by Andrei Codrescu.
Essay by Petre Răileanu.

The Big Game by Benjamin Péret *(Forthcoming)*
Translated with an introduction by Marilyn Kallet.

I Want No Part in It and Other Writings by Benjamin Péret *(Forthcoming)*
Translated with an introduction by James Brook.

Essential Poems & Writings of Jules Laforgue (Forthcoming)
Translated and edited by Patricia Terry.

MODERN POETRY SERIES

An Alchemist with One Eye on Fire by Clayton Eshleman

Archaic Design by Clayton Eshleman

Backscatter: New and Selected Poems by John Olson

Crusader-Woman by Ruxandra Cesereanu
Translated by Adam Sorkin. Introduction by Andrei Codrescu.

The Grindstone of Rapport: A Clayton Eshleman Reader
Forty Years of Verse, Translations, and Essays by Clayton Eshleman
(Forthcoming)

Forgiven Submarine by Ruxandra Cesereanu and Andrei Codrescu
(Forthcoming)

Caveat Onus by Dave Brinks
Complete cycle, four volumes combined *(Forthcoming)*

Fire Exit by Robert Kelly *(Forthcoming)*

NEW POETS SERIES

Signal from Draco: New and Selected Poems by Mebane Robertson

LITERARY THEORY/BIOGRAPHY SERIES

Revolution of the Mind: The Life of André Breton by Mark Polizzotti
Revised and augmented edition *(Forthcoming)*

WWW.BLACKWIDOWPRESS.COM